Writing in the New Nation

The Career of John Cotton:
Puritanism and the American Experience

The American 1890s:
Life and Times of a Lost Generation

Puritanism in America:
New Culture in a New World

Literary Democracy:
The Declaration of Cultural Independence in America

LARZER ZIFF

WRITING
IN THE
NEW NATION

Prose, Print, and Politics in the Early United States

Yale University Press   New Haven and London

Published with assistance from the Kingsley Trust Association Publication Fund established by the Scroll and Key Society of Yale College.

Designed by James J. Johnson and set in Fournier types by Rainsford Type, Danbury, Connecticut.

Printed in the United States of America by Vail-Ballou Press, Binghamton, New York.

Library of Congress Cataloging-in-Publication Data

Ziff, Larzer, 1927–
   Writing in the new nation : prose, print, and politics in the early United States / Larzer Ziff.
      p.   cm.
   Includes bibliographical references (p.) and index.
   ISBN 0-300-05040-2
   1. American prose literature—1783–1850—History and criticism.
   2. Politics and literature—United States—History—19th century.
   3. Politics and literature—United States—History—18th century.
   4. Literature and society—United States—History—19th century.
   5. Literature and society—United States—History—18th century.
   6. United States—Intellectual life—1783–1865.   7. Printing—United States—History.   I. Title.
PS367.Z5   1991
818'.20809—dc20   91-10291

The paper in this book meets the guidelines for permanence and durability of the Committee on Production Guidelines for Book Longevity of the Council on Library Resources.

10 9 8 7 6 5 4 3 2 1

FOR SARA AND JENNY

*Always a knit of identity . . . always distinction . . .
always a breed of life*

CONTENTS

Preface   ix
Acknowledgments   xiii

CHAPTER ONE   *The World Completed*   I
David Brainerd—Jonathan Edwards—The Prophet in Bearskins—
Immanence versus Representation

CHAPTER TWO   *The World Disrupted*   18
Writing and Self-Division in Crèvecoeur's *Farmer*—Literary Embodiment of
Revolutionary Conditions

CHAPTER THREE   *Realizing the Landscape*   34
European Rage for Ruins—American Natural History—Bartram's *Travels*—
Ordering the Exotic—Botanizing and Republicanism

CHAPTER FOUR   *Gaining Confidence*   54
Identity and Duplicity—Stephen Burroughs and Confidence—*Charlotte
Temple* and Real Property—*Arthur Mervyn* and Personal Property

CHAPTER FIVE   *Writing for Print*   83
Benjamin Franklin and Urban Experience—The *Autobiography*, Secrecy, and
Books—Print Culture and Republican Ideology

CHAPTER SIX   *Making History*   107
Adams, Jefferson, Rush: Autobiography and the Corruption of History—The
Declaration of Independence and Personality—Franklin and Representative
Autobiography—Rousseau, Emerson, and the Return of the Immanent

CHAPTER SEVEN   *The Persisting Past*   126
Thomas Jefferson and Timothy Dwight—Continuity despite Revolution—
Wieland—Irving, Cooper, and Literary Conservatism

CHAPTER EIGHT   *Captive Language*   150
Social Science and the Indian—The Lewis and Clark Expedition—Journal
versus History—Language and Captivity

CHAPTER NINE   *Wild Usages*   174
The Sensitive Frontiersman: Filson and Cooper—The Savage Frontiersman:
Brown and Bird—Wildness and Democracy: Ethan Allen—The Wild Man in
the Margin: Melville and Emerson

Afterword   193
Notes   197
Index   205

PREFACE

In the following pages I discuss the relation of literature to society in the first decades of United States history, a relation that was conceptualized by some as one between the republic of letters and the new republic. In that day, most who thought about the matter defined literature as all of written knowledge, which is to say that belles lettres constituted a very small part of what they regarded as literary. Moreover, for a number of them belles lettres were also that part of literature that was the least likely to survive in a new nation, not so much because they agreed with the zealous who argued that reading such writing weakened the moral fiber but because they believed that literature as a fine art was the creature of unjust privilege, rewarding the patronage of the ruling class by reflecting its values. They thought it unlikely that a society of free and equal men would have need for an art that, historically, had diverted the learned and leisured few while conditioning the exploited many to believe that their degraded social position was part of the natural order of things.

At the same time, however, the new republic had inherited English as its language, a medium shaped by centuries of monarchical government and carrying encoded in its diction, syntax, and especially its literary conventions the values of hierarchical society. It could not be radicalized as readily as could political institutions, although the age did not want for zany proposals toward that end. But the inherent conservatism of literary language was better met in republican society by bending literature toward a wider audience than it had ever before addressed. This did not mean the deliberate development of a popular literature, although such eventually was also to follow, so much as it meant making accessible the kind of writing that had previously been the province of a learned minority. In his *Brief Retrospect of the Eighteenth Century* (1803), which despite its title took up two dense volumes, Samuel Miller of New York noted that since the health of the republican system of government depended upon a well-informed populace, literature in the United States was descending "from the closets of philosophers, and the shelves of polite scholars, to the compting house of the merchant, to the shop of the artizan, to the bower of the husbandman, and, indeed, to every class of the community, excepting the most indigent and laborious."

This "descent" of literature was made possible by the extraordinarily rapid spread of printing presses and the consequent influence print exerted on the way reality was conceptualized. Indeed, I will argue in the following pages that print culture and American political culture were twins born from the same conditions and dependent upon one another for their well-being. To pursue this argument is to trace the ways in which literary paralleled political representation and how both in turn related to a shift in the economic sphere from real to personal—or represented—property. Such a tracing generates a consideration of the way in which the represented self contended with the immanent self both in social conduct and written narratives, a contention that on an imperial scale was repeated in the literary replacement of the actual wilderness and the living Indian with written representations that, in effect, annihilated them.

These themes, or as they are perhaps better called, these patterns, emerged from research I initially undertook on a rather imprecisely stated problem, that of the relation of literary to political culture in the period when many of the institutions of modern America received their defining shape. As I made my way into the writings of the age, I was struck by the powerful drift from immanence to representation in both literature and society, from a common belief that reality resided in a region beneath appearance and beyond manipulation to the belief that it could be constructed and so made identical with appearance. I do not mean to say that there was any moment within that period when a belief in absolute reality disappeared; if there was a drift toward representation there was always an undertow of immanence. It is observable, however, that at the outset of the period literary had been coextensive with political culture even as literature was coextensive with knowledge, while by its close the fissures that were to divide the two into separate and frequently adversarial cultures were becoming fairly evident. The division made authorship as a profession possible, but it also signaled a turn away from revolutionary, republican idealism. With such developments looming on the horizon, I close my account.

~~~~~~~~~~~~~~~~~~

Anyone who had considered the matter in the abstract could, I suppose, have told me in advance that Benjamin Franklin's *Autobiography*, say, or William Bartram's *Travels*, both of which I cite at length, would prove more rewarding than the writings of Joel Barlow or Gilbert Imlay, which I also read in detail but cite only in passing, and in pointing this out claim to have saved me a great deal of time. But it is only through having read Barlow, Imlay, and many others not cited that I was able to arrive at a sense of the pervasiveness of the patterns I trace in the exemplary texts I do discuss at length. Moreover, to approach relatively familiar works in the context of the many less familiar parallel works of their day is, in effect, to defamiliarize them and then renew them as I trust my readings will demonstrate.

Still, I admit both to some surprise at finding to how great an extent the better-recognized writers are also my best exemplars and some frustration at failing to find any good reason to display before the reader the many other writers I studied. The same condition of selection applies to fiction, where again I was surprised after reading scores of early novels to find that Charles Brockden Brown embodied the principal issues so forcefully there was no opportunity for me to cite such fascinating bores as Enos Hitchcock's *Memoirs of the Bloomsgrove Family* or so pixilated a piece of American Gothic as Isaac Mitchell's *Asylum,* which, nevertheless, I cannot here refrain from reporting, features both a castle in Connecticut complete with dungeon and a heroine who dies halfway through the tale only to reappear alive at the end because, the author explains, although she did die and was buried as he described, still since neither philosophy nor religion could reconcile the hero to her death there was no choice but to have her come to his relief in person.

Not all the works that carry the burden of my discussion, however, are so familiar as those of Franklin, Bartram, and Brown. Neither the *Memoirs* of the "notorious" Stephen Burroughs, for one example, nor Nicholas Biddle's *History of the Expedition of Lewis and Clark,* for another, is much read today, and I trust the reader of the following pages will be as pleased to encounter them as I was. For, finally, to put all theses aside, a tacit justification for this book is the vitality it finds in a group of literary works that have fallen into relative neglect. To communicate the source of their vitality is, I hope, to gain new readers for them.

ACKNOWLEDGMENTS

I have benefited from three different kinds of institutional support and offer my thanks to the Woodrow Wilson International Center for Scholars, which provided me with a fellowship that afforded time and facilities for my research; the academic administration of the Johns Hopkins University, which supports faculty research materially as well as verbally; and the Smith College Library, which extended borrowing privileges to me year after year.

Sharon Cameron extricated me from one or another of the corners in which I had penned myself and I thank her, especially because she never allowed me the easy way out. Linda Ziff commented upon the whole with her characteristic insistence upon clarity and impatience with the shallow. I am most grateful to her.

CHAPTER ONE

THE WORLD COMPLETED

David Brainerd—Jonathan Edwards—The Prophet in Bearskins—

Immanence versus Representation

O
N April 1, 1743, David Brainerd began his missionary task in the Indian village of Kaunameek, situated between Stockbridge in the Colony of Massachusetts and Albany in the Colony of New York. He was just entering upon his twenty-fifth year and to that date had given no sign that he was particularly suited for the labors he was undertaking. Indeed, it could well be conjectured that Brainerd pursued his relatively thankless duties because, given his background and character, he had little other choice.

Brainerd had been licensed to preach by the Association of Ministers of Danbury in his native Connecticut less than a year before his arrival at Kaunameek under the auspices of the Correspondents of the Society in Scotland for the Propagation of Christian Knowledge. But unlike almost all others so empowered, he held no college degree. The year before he had been expelled from Yale for ungracious conduct after having been there three years. He had entered as a twenty-one-year-old freshman, older by some three or four years than the others in his class, and this awkward circumstance seemed all too much in keeping with the previous events in his life. His father, at one time Speaker of the House in the Connecticut

Assembly and, at the time of his death when David was nine, a member of the Governor's Council, had left some farmland to his children. But there were ten of them—David was the sixth of his father's children—and whatever distinction or patrimony fell to him, buried as he was in the pack and lacking the vigor of his siblings, was heavily diluted by the time his mother died, leaving him orphaned at fourteen. When he went to East Haddam to live with his married sister he was still an adolescent, but one who, in his own words, was "something sober, and inclined rather to melancholy than the contrary extreme."[1] At no time in his subsequent brief life did he appear to emerge from this characteristic condition of morose withdrawal. The tuberculosis that killed him at age twenty-nine was accelerated by the smoke and damp of frontier bivouacs, long journeys through the wilds of the western river valleys—the Connecticut, the Delaware, the Susquehanna—and the severity of northeastern winters, and it appears to have intensified his habit of brooding retreat into himself. Brainerd seemed singularly unfit for a career that demanded some capacity to make his personal influence felt, some small power to make himself liked by strangers, some modicum of ability to look outward from his own life into the daily reality of others. It is not surprising that lacking these he was not, in practical terms, a very successful missionary.

After a year Brainerd left Kaunameek, first asking his Indian parishioners to move to Stockbridge to place themselves under the ministry of John Sargent, and in June 1744 he took up missionary work at the Forks of Delaware (near today's Easton, Pennsylvania), moving shortly afterward to an Indian settlement at Crossweeskung (near today's Freehold, New Jersey), where he enjoyed what small success in gaining converts he was to have as a missionary. By early 1747 his rapidly failing health forced him to abandon his labors, and he made his way to Northampton and the home of his fiancée, Jerusha Edwards, where tended by her he died that October.

Yet in spite of the unremarkable facts of his career, few Protestant missionaries have exerted an influence as far-reaching as David Brainerd's. He may have failed to bring significant numbers to Christianity, but his life, as transmitted in one or another published version of his diary, profoundly affected the history of Protestant missionaries. Even during his lifetime, the society that employed him published excerpts from his diary in two separate tracts, and after his death John Wesley and, more fully, Jonathan Edwards, father of his fiancée, published two of a number of other versions. The effect of these publications was momentous. Francis Asbury, who in 1771 commenced Methodism's first mission to Africa, found in the Brainerd of the diary a "Model of meekness, moderation, temptation and labor, and self-denial"; Henry Martyn, the great Anglican missionary to India, read the diary when he was a student at Cambridge in 1802 and wrote, "I long to be like him"; David Livingston, missionary to Africa, similarly responded to the diary; and as recently as 1956, the American missionary Jim Elliott, in the jungles of Ecuador on the mission which would claim his life, wrote, "Confession of pride—suggested by David Brainerd's Diary yesterday—must become an hourly thing with me."[2]

The fullest and best-known version of the diary of David Brainerd, so effective that it has come to stand as the very embodiment of the man, is that first published in Boston in 1749 by Jonathan Edwards: *An Account of the Life of the late Reverend Mr. David Brainerd, Minister of the Gospel.* Edwards's editing, fueled by both his admiration for Brainerd and the pressing political message he found in Brainerd's spiritual career, converted Brainerd's diary into the classical model it has become. Today, however, when Edwards is valued for the logic, power, and scope of his theological, philosophical, and psychological expositions, his *Life of Brainerd* is relatively unread compared with such works as his treatise on the will. But historically the *Life of Brainerd* remains the most popular of his works.

From the mid-1730s through his publication of the Brainerd life, Jonathan Edwards had been a central agent in the series of emotional religious revivals that swept through the colonies with so great an effect that they were labeled "The Great Awakening." He knew that movement was viewed with skepticism if not hostility by many leaders of the older and more polished communities of the seaboard. Indeed, Brainerd's expulsion from Yale was connected with the awakening fervor that led him to incautious behavior at a college whose president, Thomas Clap, distrusted the emotionalism of popular religious meetings as he sought to maintain a standard of intellectual decorum at his institution.[3]

Edwards further realized that since he himself had claims to membership in the colonial elite—claims based on family, education, scholarship, and native genius—his assertion that grossly physical demonstrations did not preclude the presence of grace could be viewed by many of his peers as a betrayal of his class and profession. Northampton was not so distant from London as to blur Edwards's perception of the dominant neoclassical temperament of the leading minds of his day. "Was there ever," he asked rhetorically, "an age wherein strength and penetration of reason, extent of learning, exactness of distinction, correctness of style, and clearness of expression did so abound?"[4]

Yet in the face of this recognition, he maintained that such apparently delusive and disagreeably vulgar manifestations as "trembling, groaning, being sick, crying out, panting, and fainting,"[5] comported with true religion; that, indeed, such physicality was more vitally attached to a sense of the evil of sin and the love of God than were the decorous explications of redemption that prevailed in the churches of the colonies' leaders. "Our people don't so much need to have their heads stored, as to have their hearts touched," he said, "and they stand in the greatest need of that sort of preaching that has the greatest tendency to do this" (*The Revival of Religion in New England,* p. 388).

Accordingly, he took to print in order to state his case, employing the medium traditionally controlled by the intellectual class most opposed to popular and oral, thus irresponsible and anarchic, demonstrations. His masterpiece on the subject, *A Treatise Concerning Religious Affections* (1746), was an acute psychological analysis of the connection between emotional state and physical manifestation and a model of precision in the distinctions it drew between affections generated by the imagination and those inspired by grace. It was, thus, a defense of essentially oral, subjective, emotional phenomena conducted in print according to objective, rational principles.

Edwards realized that objectifying religious experience by describing it in print presented dangers, because however precisely one formulated general psychological principles, the ultimate distinction between true and false religion resided in the particulars of the subjective experience. A failure to appreciate the details of each case led to the formulaic application of rules; led, that is, to the clogging of the vital emotional channels through which God's grace flowed. To comprehend the workings of salvation one must perforce know the particular circumstances of the life of the affected.

Accordingly, Edwards sought to supplement his psychological analyses of religious experience with a presentation of case histories. In *A Faithful Narrative of the Surprising Work of God* (1736), he reported such histories from the viewpoint of a recorder who after the event had received the spiritual details from the mouths of those shaken by grace and had talked also with those closest to them. But in Brainerd's diary he had a treasury: the extended spiritual autobiography of a Christian recorded in detail as it was experienced day by day. It was, so to speak, exactly what Edwards required to cap an argument that in other works had been advanced through a priori reasoning.

Yet read today, Brainerd's diary, personal, intense, and frequently tortured as it is, nevertheless also seems formulaic. This is because Brainerd, in common with others of his time and convictions, expresses himself in a vocabulary and according to paradigms taken principally from the Bible and then distributed in accordance with

Calvinist theology. To readers who do not inhabit his sources as familiarly as did he, Brainerd's locutions appear to be very much like those of many others, which is to say that in today's terms his highly personal document does not seem very personal at all. Only those familiar with the models that structure Brainerd's expression can detect the particularity of his agonies and his triumph.

Conversely, however, if what moved Brainerd's readers in the days of his popularity now fails similarly to impress the secular reader, there are moments in his work which formerly passed without remark that now leap from his page as indications of a structure of feeling that we discern more acutely than Brainerd precisely because we do not inhabit that structure. Such moments are often connected with the way in which the saint is separated from the sinner not only theologically but socially. In the seventeenth-century days of American Puritanism, saints were accorded political privileges and with their worldly distinction thus assured had little need to keep apart from sinners in their everyday doings. But the rekindled fervor of the Awakening occurred in the more secular days of royal governors and political preferment of a range of nominal Christians, and, as a consequence, the newly zealous sought to mark their distinction by practicing social exclusion.

So, for example, Brainerd spoke of how he marveled that those who "called themselves Christians ... could talk of all the world, and spend their time in jesting and the like and never say a word of spiritual concerns or anything of that dreadful wilderness that I had been led along through." He yearned, he said, to escape from them and "get alone in the woods, or any other place of retirement." When he contemplated what was called Christian society, he was sometimes led to think "I was a creature alone and by myself and knew not of any that felt as I did" (*Life of Brainerd,* pp. 141–42). He wrote this particular passage four years before he began missionary work, revealing in it the psychological predisposition that sent him into the literal American wilderness that corresponded to the metaphoric wilderness of his inner struggle. If Brainerd went to the wilds in order to lead the native inhabitants out of their spiritual desolation, it also appears that on a less conscious level he sought to recapture the isolation in which he had first experienced God's grace within him, an experience that could be more keenly relived among manifest pagans than among those he saw as the hypocrites of Christian society.

On a Sunday two weeks after his arrival at Kaunameek Brainerd wrote:

> In the morning was again distressed as soon as I waked, hearing much talk about the world and the things of it: Though I perceived the men were in some measure afraid of me; and I discoursed something about sanctifying the Sabbath, if possible, to solemnize their minds. But when they were at a little distance, they again talked freely about secular affairs. Oh, I thought, what a hell it would be to live with such men to eternity. (*Life of Brainerd,* p. 204)

The anticipated bliss of the social exclusiveness to be enjoyed in eternity feeds Brainerd's distaste for the society this world affords. He also perceives that his clerical garb, his sober demeanor, and his unrelenting attention to spiritual decorum make him an object of fear, and it is this perception that provides the most extraordinary passage in his diary.

On September 21, 1745, a Lord's Day, Brainerd visited the Indians encamped on Juniata Island in the Susquehanna and attempted to gather them together in order to preach to them through an interpreter. But he found them so fully engaged in ceremonies designed to counter a fever then raging among them that they paid him no heed. Watching the ceremonies, Brainerd wrote, "Their monstrous actions tended to excite ideas of horror, and seemed to have something in them (as I thought) peculiarly suited to raise the devil, if he could be raised by anything odd, ridiculous, and frightful" (*Life of Brainerd,* p. 327). Waiting out the powwow for some three hours, he resumed his attempt to talk to them about Christianity, but they soon scattered, leaving him so "greatly sunk" in spirits that he thought the day "the most burdensome and disagreeable Sabbath that ever I saw" (p. 328). In this depressed condition, he recalled and recorded an incident that had occurred some months earlier. Its singularity merits quotation in full:

When I was in these parts in May last, I had an opportunity of learning many of the notions and customs of the Indians, as well as of observing many of their practices: I then travelling more than an hundred and thirty miles upon the river above the English settlements; and having in that journey a view of some persons of seven or eight distinct tribes, speaking so many different languages. But of all the sights I ever saw among them, or indeed anywhere else, none appeared so frightful or so near akin to what is usually imagined of infernal powers; none ever excited such images of terror in my mind, as the appearance of one who was a devout and zealous reformer, or rather restorer, of what he supposed was the ancient religion of the Indians. He made his appearance in his pontifical garb, which was a coat of bears' skins, dressed with the hair on, and hanging down to his toes, a pair of bearskin stockings, and a great wooden face, painted the one half black, the other tawny, about the color of an Indian's skin, with an extravagant mouth, cut very much awry; the face fastened to a bearskin cap which was drawn over his head. He advanced toward me with the instrument in his hand that he used for music in his idolatrous worship, which was a dry tortoiseshell, with some corn in it, and the neck of it drawn on to a piece of wood, which made a very convenient handle. As he came forward he beat his tune with the rattle, and danced with all his might, but did not suffer any part of his body, not so much as his fingers, to be seen: And no man would have guessed by his appearance and actions that he could have been a human creature if they had not had some intimation of it otherways. When he came near me I could not but shrink away from him, although it was then noonday, and I knew who it was, his appearance and gestures were so prodigiously frightful! He had a house consecrated to religious uses, with divers images cut out upon the several parts of it. I went in and found the ground beat almost as hard as a rock with their frequent dancing in it. I discoursed with him about Christianity, and some of my discourse he seemed to like; but some of it he disliked entirely. He told me that God had taught him his religion, and that he never would turn from it, but wanted to find some that would join heartily with him in it; for the Indians, he said, were grown very degenerate and corrupt. He had thoughts, he said, of leaving all his friends and travelling abroad, in order to find some that would join him; for he believed God had some good people somewhere that felt as he did. He had not always, he said, felt as he now did, but had formerly been like the rest of the Indians, until about four or five years before that time: Then, he said, his heart was very much distressed, so that he could not live among the Indians, but got away into the woods and lived alone for some months. At length, he says, God comforted his heart and showed him what he should do; and since that time he had known God and tried to serve him; and loved all men, be they who they would, so as he never did before. He treated me with uncommon courtesy, and seemed to be hearty in it. And I was told by the Indians that he opposed their drinking strong liquor with all his power; and if at any time he could not dissuade them from it, by all he could say, he would leave them and go crying into the woods. It was manifest he had a set of religious notions that he had looked into for himself, and not taken for granted upon bare tradition; and he relished or disrelished whatever was spoken of a religious nature, according as it either agreed or disagreed with his standard. And while I was discoursing he would sometimes say, "Now that I like; so God has taught me," etc. And some of his sentiments seemed very just. Yet he utterly denied the being of a devil, and declared there was no such a creature known among the Indians of old times, whose religion he supposed he was attempting to revive. He likewise told me that departed souls all went southward, and that the difference between the good and the bad was this: that the former were ad-

mitted into a beautiful town with spiritual walls, or walls agreeable
to the nature of souls; and that the latter would forever hover round
those walls, and in vain attempt to get in. He seemed to be sincere,
honest and conscientious in his own way, and according to his own
religious notions, which was more than I ever saw in any other
pagan: And I perceived he was looked upon and derided amongst
most of the Indians as a precise zealot that made a needless noise
about religious matters. But I must say there was something in his
temper and disposition that looked more like true religion than
anything I ever observed amongst other heathens. (*Life of Brainerd,*
pp. 329–30)

On an island at the junction of the Juniata and Susquehanna rivers,
David Brainerd had met his double.[6] Both men had undergone profound religious conversions which had launched them on their mis-
sions; both strove to make every outward appearance comport with
the spiritual truth revealed to them; both were regarded by their
fellows as tiresome precisians at best and objects of fear at worst.
In covering himself in bear skins, the Indian prophet emphasized
his total difference from the encroaching Europeans who were contributing to the degeneration of his fellows and at the same time he
symbolized the regenerative forces available for the redemption of
his fellows. Like the bear skins, Brainerd's clerical garb at the same
time emphasized his total difference from an opposed culture and
symbolized the redemptive force available to those who adhered to
his culture. For a magic moment a charge of identity surged between
the two missionaries as they recognized that the similar demands
made by their gods suggested their kinship.

But Brainerd, as fearful spiritually of the shaman's similarity to
him as he had earlier been fearful physically of the shaman's difference, sought to distance himself from the Indian and found the
way in their opposing views not on God but on the question of the
devil's existence. Within Brainerd's demonology, to deny the reality
of the devil was to serve him. In insisting upon their difference,

however, Brainerd did not dismiss the shaman into his own culture, granting him a separate if different identity. Rather, he held him fast within the Christian myth, an example of the devil's sway among the heathens, a theological role that blended with the cultural role of the savage. Both were parts of the Christian American's drama of identity wherein the repressed yet luring self was externalized and then attacked.[7]

In seeking to revive what he regarded as the true old Indian religion, the shaman sought also to revive his fellows' national identity, to restore them to a sense of what it meant to be a Delaware and an Indian uncompromised by European habits. In seeking to convert the Indians he visited, Brainerd was annihilating their cultural identity by subordinating it to the roles they had to play in his cosmic Christian drama. As the shaman's mission was national, so Brainerd's was imperial.[8] To convert the heathen was to be an agent of providential history, an instrument in the working out of God's predetermined plan for the world. Although one could not be certain as to the precise place in God's script at which one had arrived at a given historical moment, still the Bible provided a clear scenario for the whole plot from the creation to the apocalypse. America was the designated site for prescribed acts in the drama of the history of the world, a drama which would achieve its climax only after the conversion of the heathen. The Indian prophet, on the other hand, in his attempt to return to (or maintain) the world that prevailed before the European invasion, appears to have held a view of history as essentially complete, although from the slimness of the evidence we can only conjecture this. Such a view accounted for the arrival of the European by reading him back into the period before the invasion in terms of signs that had anticipated his presence.

Discussing the Aztecs' absorption of the Spanish conquest into their history, Tzvetan Todorov writes: "The Aztecs perceive the conquest—i.e., the defeat—and at the same time, mentally overcome it by inscribing it within a history conceived according to their requirements (nor are they the only people to have done such a thing): the present becomes intelligible and at the same time less inadmissible, the moment one can see it already announced in the past. And the remedy is so well adapted to the situation that, hearing the narrative, everyone believes he remembers that the omens had indeed appeared *before* the conquest."[9] To cite this is not to assert an identity between sixteenth-century Aztecs and eighteenth-century Delawares in gross perpetuation of the irresponsible habit of lumping all Indian people from all preinvasion times into a homogeneous mass.[10] It is, rather, to provide a well-observed example of the way in which a view of history as always complete, always, that is, having fulfilled the divine plan, can incorporate into it the evidence of "new" events instead of giving way to a linear view of history as change.

Strikingly, once the contrast between a view of history as linear and a view of it as complete is noted, then a similarity between Puritan and Indian presents itself. The theory of providential history arose from a reading of the New Testament in a way encouraged by the testament itself, one that saw the advent of Jesus as a fulfillment of what had already been written in the Old Testament. In a like manner, the future history of the world is already patterned forth in the New Testament, so that what will occur tomorrow can, once it happens, be related to its reference in the Bible in a procedure not unlike the reading of omens after the fact.

The intellectual habit of seeing the world as complete even as it unfolds, of, that is, finding an already occurred double for what is just now occurring, is manifest in the writings of Jonathan Edwards published in the same period as his edition of the *Life of Brainerd.* In *Some Thoughts Concerning the Revival of Religion in New England* (1742), for example, he wrote: "God has made as it were two worlds here below, the old and the new (according to the names they are now called by), two great habitable continents.... This new world is probably now discovered that the new and most glorious state of God's church on earth might commence there; that God might in it begin a new world in a spiritual respect when he creates the *new heavens* and the *new earth.*" He went on to treat America as a geographical correlative of the New Testament: "The other continent hath slain Christ, and has from age to age shed the blood of the saints and martyrs of Jesus, and has often been as it were deluged with the Church's blood: God has therefore probably reserved the honor of building the glorious temple to the daughter, that has not shed so much blood, when those times of the peace and prosperity and glory of the church shall commence, that were typified by the reign of Solomon." The last world to be "discovered," America will be the first world to experience the coming of the days of glory. "'Tis probable that that will come to pass in spirituals," Edwards said, "that has in temporals, with respect to America; that whereas, till of late, the world was supplied with its silver and gold and earthly treasures from the old continent, now it's supplied chiefly from the new, so the course of things in spiritual respects will be in like manner turned" (*The Revival of Religion in New England,* p. 355).

Seeing America as the realization of what has unalterably been determined imparted a cosmic consequence to the lives of ordinary people. Their spiritual experiences became events in world history; what happened in a church revival in a remote part of the colonies was a step in the progress of the divine plan for the universe. The common man could see himself as a participant in matters of far greater public consequence than those that were managed by his social betters in the commercial and political centers of the land. The text that accompanied Edwards's message about the role of America was one that consistently relocated authority, taking it from its traditional places and lodging it in the lowly believer.

"When God is about to do some great work for his church," he wrote, "his manner is to begin at the lower end; so when he is about to renew the whole habitable earth, 'tis probable that he will begin in this utmost, meanest, youngest and weakest part of it, where the church of God has been planted last of all; and so the first shall be last, and the last first" (*The Revival of Religion in New England,* p. 356). The immediate referent of "this utmost . . . weakest part" is America, where the church was "planted last" after its Near Eastern origin and European development. Beyond that referent, however, lies another to the churches of Edwards's frontier as youngest and weakest when compared to those of the Atlantic seaboard, and beyond this lies a third to the socially lowest members of the church as opposed to the socially dominant who have not experienced an awakening. His text denies the subordination of colonial American to imperial English culture, of frontier to capital society, of lower to upper class. While his explicit terms limit the relocation of power to spiritual matters, at the same time they declare that such are the greatest matters in history. So thorough is Edwards's relocation of power that it extends even to his own authority. "I condemn," he said, "ministers' assuming or taking too much upon them, and appearing as though they supposed that they were the persons to whom it especially belonged to dictate, direct and determine" (p. 291), and he took care to dissociate himself from such behavior.

It can be argued that Edwards's emphasis on the spiritual authority of the believer prepared his followers for the revolution in which they assumed political authority, a revolution Edwards did not live to see. But that revolution and the republic that succeeded it were, as will be seen, preeminently creatures of print culture while Edwards's outlook is shaped by the assumptions of oral culture.

At the root of the American Puritan tradition was the belief that the presence of the Holy Spirit in the believer took precedence over laws, that the divine influence was experienced as a flow rather than through forms. The presence of the Word was a necessary precondition for the efficacy of words; the Holy Spirit had written the Bible and only those who had that Spirit knew how to read the Bible. As John Calvin had said, "Scripture, carrying its own evidence along with it, deigns not to submit to proofs and arguments but owes the full conviction with which we ought to receive it to the testimony of the Spirit."[11] In everyday terms this resulted in a heavy emphasis placed on spontaneity in preaching and prayer, and a deep suspicion of set forms since they were seen as hollow substitutes for, rather than the outgrowth of, the presence of the Spirit. By Edwards's time, however, Puritanism had had some five generations of existence as the way of the establishment rather than the way of dissent, and the emphasis on spontaneity had been modified by codes of decorum. The Great Awakening was a popular reaction against the spiritual authority of the ministerial class and its allies who exerted their control through the maintenance of forms that they were especially qualified by training to administer. It was the rebellion of an oral culture valuing immanence against a literary culture valuing representation.

Jonathan Edwards recognized, to be sure, that no matter how valid the insistence upon immanence—the living presence of the Holy Spirit—and the distrust of representation—the investing of authority in laws of conduct and a class that administered them— the resulting fervor could grow into a wildfire of delusion. Anarchic behavior might be justified by claims that since the Holy Spirit authorized it all rules to the contrary were inapplicable. The chaos that threatened was not, he perceived, to be checked by attacking the anarchic behavior itself; indeed, to do so would be to align himself with the Awakening's opponents who impugned the integrity of spiritual experience by deriding its outer manifestations. Rather, since the Holy Spirit was always consistent with itself so that its presence in an individual could lead neither to conduct that was in conflict with the conduct of another individual equally guided nor to conflict with the words of the Bible that it had written, when such conflict appeared to occur it was not the behavior itself but its sources that required analysis. It is not correct, he agreed, to judge of the truth of the presence of the Spirit by the way a Christian conducts himself; to do so is to put the law in the place of grace. But it is necessary to recognize that certain standards of conduct— he called them "holy practice"—inevitably followed from the profession of grace (*Religious Affections,* pp. 458–59). The created world is determined, not subject to re-creation. When the consciousness is awakened by grace it sees that world in a new light, as if one previously blind to color now saw all its hues. But it does not see, nor is it empowered to create, a different world. The divine plan still dictates that the world is as it is and shall be as it shall be, independently of human will.

Accordingly, Edwards centered his analysis on the ways grace is to be distinguished from the imagination, which seems like but in truth is completely different from it. The imagination is the faculty Satan employs to delude persons into repeating his own revolt by leading them to believe they have the power to affirm a new order. The greater part of Edwards's attention in his *Religious Affections* was devoted to exposing the imagination as the source of experiences that were mistakenly regarded as inspired by grace, and in his editing of the Brainerd diary he omitted visions that Brainerd recorded when he suspected them to be products of the imagination.

Edwards's belief that the created world was complete and his consequent censure of imaginative re-creations are opposed to the values promoted in a print culture. The first novels to be published in America appeared in the same decade as Edwards's writings in defense of the Great Awakening, the very first of them Samuel Richardson's *Pamela* printed by Benjamin Franklin in 1740. The rapid increase in the number of novels published in America signaled the coming of age of print culture. Unlike poetry and drama, the novel is preeminently a product of the printing press. Although connected to oral story telling, the novel is, uniquely, written only to be printed. Its popularity in a society is a mark of the degree to which that society's perceptions are shaped by the assumptions that govern print. The coincidence of Edwards's popular influence reaching its highest point in the decade when the novel commenced its entry into American life suggests that the oral culture that had empowered Edwards's writings had reached flood point and was soon to ebb.

David Brainerd's self was his God-given soul, and his drama was the drama of coming to terms with that given. It was a drama of self-awareness. The new culture of print promoted one's ability to be what one represented oneself as being. It replaced self-awareness with self-knowledge. As Ormond Seavey wrote in studying Benjamin Franklin, "In place of the dramatic possibilities made available by self-awareness, self-knowledge organized life narratively, in the manner of novels or autobiographies."[12]

The transition from a culture of immanence to a culture of representation is a central feature of the writings that are considered in the following pages, writings framed by Crèvecoeur's *Letters from an American Farmer* and the journals of Meriwether Lewis and William Clark. Personal narratives, travel accounts, natural histories, and novels are read with an eye to what they capture of the relation of literary to other forms of representation, the construction of self in writing, and the conquest of the wild through letters, themes that recurred in the literature of a people who were consolidating the first modern republic. So to read these texts is to seek to enter into their historical reality rather than to reconstruct it, although, to be sure, any contention about the way in which those in a past period perceived reality is vulnerable to the objection that if the work being interpreted is bound by the historical situation of its author then the interpretation is bounded by the historical situation of the interpreter.[13] This is undoubtedly so. But the recognition that our perception of reality is inescapably shaped by our times stimulates a desire to enter into the consciousness of the people of an earlier period rather than discourages such an attempt. To arrive at a sense of another day is to interrogate today.

CHAPTER TWO

THE WORLD DISRUPTED

Writing and Self-Division in Crèvecoeur's *Farmer*—Literary Embodiment of

Revolutionary Conditions

ETTERS FROM AN AMERICAN FARMER was published in London in 1782, the year after its author, Michel Guillaume St. Jean de Crèvecoeur, had deposited the manuscript with the printer as he passed through the city en route from America to France. The book consists of twelve chapters—called "Letters" although the epistolary convention is employed only as a general framework—eleven of which combine to provide the most memorable of all literary images of eighteenth-century rural America as well as a classic discussion of the promise of America, what came to be called the American dream. Crèvecoeur appears to have worked consciously to elevate his work to the definitive status it achieved, since in addition to providing descriptions of occupations, manners, and landscapes from Nantucket to Charleston, he also related the physical to the social and economic scene in a consideration of the way the new world conferred a new identity. He was the first writer to raise the question "What is an American?" in exactly those words, and in his third letter, devoted explicitly to the topic, he conceptualized national identity in terms of the shaping force of material and political opportunity rather than, as had been common up to this point, simply in terms of ethnicity, religion, or political allegiance. Although Crèvecoeur's concept of America as a social force capable of erasing old-world distinctions came to be the dominant element in the self-image Americans held for more than a century after he enunciated it, his own experience was more strongly and more darkly marked by the dissolution of such an America back into the conflicting parts he claimed it would blend into a new identity.[1]

Born into the petty nobility of Normandy, Crèvecoeur emigrated to Canada where at the close of the French and Indian Wars he served under Montcalm. Attracted by the relative liberality of British rule, however—he had spent some years in England—he readily accepted if not actually welcomed its extension in North America, and after the defeat of the French he traveled in Pennsylvania and New York, gained naturalization as a British subject, married, in 1769, a woman with a ringingly Yankee name, Mehitabel Tippett, purchased land in Orange County, New York, and there began to improve a farm that he named Pine Hill. By this time he had anglicized his name to J. Hector St. John, a sign of the new identity he was crystallizing as the farmer of Pine Hill and idealizing in the book upon which he worked while improving his lands. In the seven years following his marriage, St. John fathered three children, saw his prosperity increase with the increase to his family, and established warm social relations with his neighbors on both sides of the nearby Hudson River. French ancestry, British liberties, and an ample land's provision both of bread for labor and leisure in which to write combined to make him neither French nor British but what he called "this new man," the American.

As colonial discontents moved toward a revolutionary war, however, St. John found himself unable to take sides. His idealization of America was based on a personal freedom he regarded as secured by British rule and threatened by the rebellious populace. At the same time, he could not contemplate continued residence on his farm as a loyalist because his idealization of America was also based on his sense of community, and he was, as a consequence, repelled by the notion of being violently opposed to his neighbors. With the American condition disintegrating, he concluded that the wisest move would be to return to France and there acquire for his children whatever was theirs by birthright as Crèvecoeurs. Accordingly, in 1778 he made his way to British-occupied New York City in order to find passage back to France. But while distrust of his revolutionary neighbors had impelled Crèvecoeur to New York, the British authorities' distrust of him as a possible rebel detained him there. Not until September 1780 was he allowed to embark, and then he encountered yet another obstacle in the form of the blockading fleet his fellow Frenchmen maintained in support of the Americans. So completely had his literary conflation of personal with social identity been destroyed by events that it is not surprising that he suffered a nervous breakdown in 1779. Contrary to his most cherished belief, French, British, and American proved, after all, to be distinct entities, each opposed to the others and all opposed to him. Finally, Crèvecoeur did get back to France, on the way leaving the *Letters* with a London publisher, and when he returned to New York in 1783 he did so as Louis XVI's counsel, an eminent man not because he held the post but because of the fame he had gained as the author of the *Letters*.

The biographical account provides a strong extratextual explanation for the radical unevenness that all readers and admirers of Crèvecoeur's book detect in it. A work that pleasantly and persuasively combines pastoral idyll, shrewd social observation, and charming protomythic details of natural history suddenly and violently collapses at its very close into a nightmare that, in formal literary terms, has not been prepared. The penultimate letter begins with the expansive and relaxed tone characteristic of the greater part of the preceding ones: "Examine this flourishing province in what light you will, the eye as well as the mind of an European traveller are equally delighted because a diffusive happiness appears in every part, happiness which is established on the broadest basis" (*Letters,* p. 187). It closes with the same glow, mentioning "golden days," "gratitude," and "immeasurable kindnesses" (p. 199). Yet we turn the page to the final letter and begin, "I wish for a change of place; the hour is come at last that I must fly from my house and abandon my farm" (p. 200), and we are plunged into the horrors of a civil war that the loyalist farmer, not wanting further to exasperate his republican neighbors, displaces into the terms of the terrors of the Indian warfare that has erupted as a consequence of the political conflict. In this twelfth letter, both physical and mental scenes are places of torment. The reader feels suddenly dislocated because nowhere earlier was there a discussion of the political differences that led to the war, and, indeed, even in the final letter the political issues are so buried that it takes a while to ascertain the cause of the extreme psychic distress of the writing farmer.

If, then, the *Letters from an American Farmer* are, as many have observed, the first and in some ways still the definitive expression of the American dream, they also express an American nightmare. The stuff of dream is the identical stuff of nightmare because the dream proceeds from the perception that in America one's lot in life is not governed by a principle extrinsic to the will—one can emerge from what in Europe was inherited poverty and powerlessness into substance and authority and in so doing not only create oneself but make the society in which such opportunity is constantly available. Correspondingly, however, since there is no American world other than that one makes, the failure of that world represents the collapse of the self.

The standard reading of Crèvecoeur's *Letters* was established by Moses Coit Tyler, who in 1897 saw the book as a mirror of colonial life on the eve of the Revolution and who first called attention to those vignettes that make the book an enduring pleasure. Tyler recognized that all in it was not cheerful and remarked that "by its inclusion of [some] . . . sombre and agonizing aspects of life in America, the book gains, as is most obvious, both in authenticity and in literary strength." But, Tyler insisted, despite the dark moments and the nightmare chapter with which the *Letters* concludes, "the reader is tempted to infer that, after all, felicity is the permanent fact there, and that suffering is but a temporary accident."[2]

One cannot quarrel with this account if it is read in the light of Tyler's assumption that literary history is the inner history of outward events, that it measures texts in terms of their relation to a reality external to them. Although the horrified vision of widespread ruin in the farmer's last letter is sharply different from most of what precedes it, our knowledge of what actually happened historically after the moment at which the book closes can lead us, if we follow Tyler's assumptions, to subordinate the nightmare to what he calls a permanent felicity.

If, however, we entertain the hypothesis that the *Letters* constitutes a reality rather than reflects one that existed independently of it, then we are alert to a concern that is psychologically and intellectually present from the book's earliest pages.[3] We can then see that the eruption of physical conflict at the close is an externalization of irreconcilable differences within the writer's position rather than the intrusion of public events into an otherwise felicitous private life. These differences exist as a conflict between what is valorized in the writing and the act of writing itself. To read the *Letters* as an embodiment of a cultural reality rather than a picture of external reality is to deny the gap between private circumstance and public event. The revolution did not happen to the farmer; his self-division was a part of it.

Prior to the nightmarish conclusion, the individual letters, with one exception, maintain an air of unforced cheer as their author depicts life in the colonies and, most memorably, the domestic economy of his farm. Detail after detail leaves the page as words and is retained in the memory as a scene from a perfect life. In the winter the farmer sees the quail, tamed by hunger, mingling with his barnyard fowl: "Often in the angles of the fences where the motion of the wind prevents the snow from settling, I carry them both chaff and grain, the one to feed them, the other to prevent their tender feet from freezing fast to the earth as I have frequently observed them to do" (*Letters,* pp. 56–57). The wren, the swallow, and the phoebe each has her box on his piazza where he observes them as he smokes his contemplative pipe. When the wren leaves her box to usurp that of the swallow, he muses, "Where did this little bird learn the spirit of injustice? It was not endowed with what we term reason!" (p. 63). But the farmer is so endowed, and he moves the wren's box to another part of the house rather than repay violence with violence.

Plenty for all who want and room for each to live according to his nature cohere in an all-embracing harmony. There is nothing on the farm that cannot be brought into tune. "The curious republic of industrious hornets" whose nest balloons from a twig hanging in the parlor repays hospitality in an unforgettable way. Feeding on troublesome flies "they are constantly busy in catching them, even on the eyelids of my children" (p. 63). The domestic animals also cohere into the imposed pattern of giving and receiving, their plumpness a source of pride not only to the farmer but, one is moved to believe, to themselves. The fat and happy horses gratefully pulling the plow on the handles of which the farmer has seated his baby son seem to glide down the furrow as in a painting by Hicks, their blimplike bodies serving to lift their legs and float them along the ground. Meanwhile, the farmer's wife sits knitting under a tree at the edge of the field, "praising the straightness of my furrow and the docility of my horses" (p. 52).

Within such a scene increase promotes increase and happiness is assured. The shade that frames the brightness of the picture is the realization that across the ocean there are common men like the farmer who do not own their own soil but drudge on hopelessly. The only increase they experience is the birth of children, and this that should be cause for joy only augments wretchedness. "In America, with its abundant resources, every man feels the increase of his family to be the increase of his riches," wrote Gilbert Imlay in echo of Crèvecoeur.[4] America is that place on earth in which fecund nature welcomes the fecundity of humans.

The exception to the series of memorable scenes of harmony occurs when the farmer visits Charleston and is staggered by the treatment of slaves there. He too keeps Negroes, but, he feels, they are blended into the pervasive harmony as a cooperative part of the farm. The very different condition of the slave in South Carolina is fixed, in Crèvecoeur's characteristic fashion, in a picture that emblematizes his feeling. On a walk in the Carolina woods, the farmer encounters a slave who is being punished by being suspended in a cage hung from a tree where he shall remain until he expires. He has become so weak that the birds have pecked out his eyes and are attacking other parts of his body. The man in the cage begs to be killed, and the farmer confesses, "Had I a ball in my gun I certainly should have dispatched him." Instead, after giving the man a cup of water he retreats in disgust: "Humanity herself would have recoiled back with horror" (*Letters,* p. 178).

The center of revulsion is the pecking birds, signifying a nature out of joint with man because man has placed himself athwart it. In all the happy scenes that predominate in the other places viewed, people work and thus cooperate with nature. But in the slave states the owners of the soil have consigned to slaves the labor that would integrate them with their land.

Throughout the *Letters* free labor is happiness; it is not so much that people are happy because they work but that they express their happiness in work. Labor is their clearest and cleanest expression of their relation to their world—a poetry of action. But where people own neither the soil on which they labor nor the result of their labors, they do not express themselves by their work but are crippled, made mute, oppressed by it. Within an economy in which labor is the role of a separate landless class—and here one is tempted to read slavery in South Carolina as an extension of the peasantry system in Europe—expression too is detached from all in the society and specialized into art by the class that profits from the labor of others. Such perceptions reside beneath the surface of Crèvecoeur's text, and the genuine joy he finds in his America—geographically, Pennsylvania; abstractly, the place where a penniless person can gain land as a reward for work—is a function of its amplitude relative to its population far more than of its civil polity.[5] So long as people can enjoy the fruits of their labor, which is also freedom to express themselves in labor itself, it matters little who is king. And so the fratricidal fuss about that very matter repels the writer of the *Letters*.

But repelled as he may be by that conflict, he is implicated in its causes; he is not just a sufferer of its effects. Political neutrality may be possible, but cultural neutrality is not.

~~·eccereeeQaaauaaa·~~

Crèvecoeur's essays descriptive of American life are called "letters" because in a fiction established in the first of them they are written in Pennsylvania by a farmer named James to a Mr. F. B. in London at F. B.'s request. He is, we learn, a great man who has traveled widely in Europe as well as having made a tour to America at which time he met James. This epistolary fiction broadens the actual contrast between Crèvecoeur, the cultured farmer, and his European readership into one between a far simpler husbandman and a specific English reader who is wealthy and cosmopolitan, the better to point up the capacity of American conditions to elevate the character. Although the literary convention of letters from the country to the city had a long history, within that convention it had previously been understood that the countryman or farmer who wrote to the city was a gentleman, an educated person who knew the city well, had visited if not lived there, and now resided rurally from preference rather than necessity. The praise of the country presented in the letter was very often part of a larger criticism of city ways. James, however, is a laboring not a gentleman farmer, and his praise of American farm life makes no extended reference to city life in America or England. Insofar as a contrast is offered, it is to the life of the British peasant, a laborer of origins similar to James's who, were he to come to America, would become James's neighbor and equal. James's is a voice not before heard in literature, and he is acutely conscious of the fact.

"Who would have thought," his first letter begins, "that because I received you with hospitality and kindness, you should imagine me capable of writing with propriety and perspicuity? Your gratitude misleads your judgment" (*Letters,* p. 39). He goes on to disqualify himself: his heart, it is true, is warm, but his mind is limited; his knowledge does not extend beyond farming; he has had little education and what few books he owns he possesses not because he purchased them but because he inherited them from his father who brought them from England when he emigrated; he never has written and can summon up no language appropriate to the task of writing. James's wife, moreover, when told of F. B.'s request ("and I never do anything without consulting her," he says) laughs in his face at the idea that he would "pretend to letter it" with a man who studied at Cambridge and traveled so widely that he has even, as she says, "seen the factory of brimstone at 'Suvius" (p. 40).

So James attempts to transfer the task to the only lettered person he knows, his minister, and it is the minister's response that persuades him to undertake it himself. Write as you speak, the minister advises, and talk only about what lies within the reach of your experience because that is what F. B. wants to hear. His extensive travels in places such as Italy will not lead him to be disappointed with the less exotic details of American life. Quite the contrary, says the minister, who then launches into an argument on behalf of the superiority of America to Italy as an object of contemplation. The farmer is persuaded and resolves upon the letters despite his wife's continuing objections, which, significantly, switch from contentions about James's being unqualified to write the letters to forebodings of the dire consequences that will follow when news spreads among their neighbors that he is engaged in such foolishness.

With these preliminaries out of the way, the descriptive letters commence and wife and minister disappear as characters. James's style is not markedly colloquial as he ranges beyond his immediate experience in the spectrum of topics that follows his consideration of the situation of the typical American farmer: descriptions of life at Nantucket, Martha's Vineyard, and Charleston; an extended description of the character of the noted botanist, John Bartram, a Pennsylvania farmer who did, in fact, "letter it" with great personages in Europe; and, famously, a discussion of the question "What is an American?" The fiction of the opening scene serves to get things going and then seems no longer to be a factor in the *Letters*. But if our interest is in the reality constituted by the *Letters* rather than any reality presumed to be external to and reflected by it, then James's wife does not disappear without leaving behind the powerful specter of her views.

Her initial objection to the letter writing arises from her sense of a vast discrepancy between James's simplicity and the sophistication of his correspondent. But as she warms to her argument, she shows greater concern for the social and political implications of James's act. If the neighbors learned of his letter writing he would be accused of "idleness and vain notions not befitting [his] condition." More ominously, "our colonel," the local magistrate,

> would be often coming here to know what it is that thee canst write so much about. Some would imagine that thee wantest to become an assemblyman or a magistrate, which God forbid, and that thee art telling the king's men abundance of things. Instead of being well looked upon as now, and living in peace with all the world, our neighbours would be making strange surmises; I had rather be as

we are, neither better nor worse than the rest of our country folks. (*Letters,* p. 48)

Despite the apolitical purpose of those letters on local manners and natural history, they could be regarded by the Crown's agents as subversive and by the neighbors as antisocially ambitious. What is at issue, of course, is not *what* James writes but *that* he writes. From the authorities' viewpoint, a writing farmer indicates a disordering of the hierarchy on which political stability rests; from the neighbors' viewpoint a farmer writing indicates that there is in their midst one who is other than what he seems to be.

The James who works on his farm, goes to church, and participates in town meetings is known to himself and others through his personal presence. To put in the place of this James one who is abstracted onto paper in language, a represented rather than an immanent self, is to fragment a present, natural wholeness. James's wife says:

> Great people over sea may write to our townsfolk because they have nothing else to do. These Englishmen are strange people; because they can live upon what they call bank notes, without working, they think that all the world can do the same.... But if they have no trees to cut down, they have gold in abundance, they say, for they rake and scrape it from all parts far and near. I have often heard my grandfather tell how they live there by writing. By writing they send this cargo unto us, that to the West, and the other to the East Indies. (pp. 48–49)

Here, of course, the writing that is so distrusted is extended to commercial paper and the attendant documents of trade. But it is not distinguished from the kind of uncommercial epistles James is being asked to compose because the abstraction of James's written self from his immanent self parallels the translation of the farmer's labor into the paper wealth of the merchant.

Paper currency expedited the incorporation of the farmer into a market economy.[6] His farm and his labor acquired a value represented by such paper, which was different from the value he assigned it. As the farmer increasingly participated in the market system, so he became more separated from the values that were once central to his life and that Crèvecoeur's *Letters* celebrates. Although the book is not explicitly concerned with such matters, James's wife suspects a connection and she perceives, however obscurely, that her husband's commitment to writing—to his represented rather than his immanent self—somehow shadows the operation of commercial paper.

Writing can overcome distance as speech cannot, and it does so at the expense of the community knit together by personal presence. James's writing means the end of the world he will glorify in his letters because it displaces expression from the living of the daily life to written words. Once the happy farmer becomes the writing farmer he disrupts the harmony he intends to celebrate. If he can abstract himself from his everyday presence and assume a practice that is traditionally that of another class, then despite his political loyalty to the British system he is manifesting the cultural circumstance that disrupts it.

In the letter of distress that closes the book, James, determined to fight neither neighbor nor royal government, must flee his farm either to the city, where he will presumably be protected from actual battle by royal troops, or the frontier, where he will presumably be beyond the range of warfare. His principal concern is for his children, and with that in mind he elects the frontier and settlement near some Indians he previously befriended. As brutish as he had earlier found their life to be—he, for one, had no doubts that the Indians were savages and that those English who before the war sought their company were the dregs of society—he has a greater fear of the effects on his children of the city since he sees it as vicious in manner because removed from nature and the common impulses of humanity. There on the frontier he intends to clear land and start a new farm in replication of the process that his grandfather had followed when he immigrated to America, so that by war's end he and his sons will have reestablished the conditions that prevailed in the happy farm he was forced to flee.

But though he elected the frontier over the city, he is, nevertheless, unable to escape the economically determined culture of the detested city. In the absence of markets, he realizes, his sons will have no incentive to labor for more than subsistence, and so, he fears, will be attracted to the Indians' manner of living by the hunt rather than by agriculture. He must hold them to industriousness in excess of their immediate needs in order to prevent their barbarizing. "I will keep an exact account of all that shall be gathered," he says, "and give each of them a regular credit for the amount of it, to be paid them in real property at the return of peace" (p. 223). Although he thinks to reproduce the condition of his former felicity, another seed has been sown and he must now govern his family with paper. Before the war, what he calls "real property" had preceded the paper money which was but a representation of it. Now represented property will precede real in a reversal that makes the real the represented.

The harmony of the natural and social worlds the farmer enjoyed on his Pennsylvania farm was the result of a balance maintained between two worlds, that of unmediated contact with abundant American nature, symbolized by the Indians, and that of the profits of the market, symbolized by the city. His farm was a middle ground that took the better part of each of the opposing grounds and left the worse part of each, savagery on one hand, the vices of luxury on the other. From his viewpoint, the war was something that happened as the result of causes in which he had no part, and once it was over the middle ground would again be available for the winning.

He was not alone in his belief. In his study of what he terms "the American revolution against patriarchal authority, 1750–1800,"

Jay Fliegelman points out the connection between such an ideal and the disappearance of belief in the formative influence of innate ideas in favor of a belief in the shaping influence of the impressions the undetermined mind receives from the senses. "In its emphatic insistence on the need to separate from a fatal European corruption," he says, "the rhetoric of the American revolution would wishfully describe America as the world's last refuge" from the "terrifying vulnerability" of being at the mercy of "uncontrollable impressions, distractions, and random events." It would insist upon the need for Americans "to seal the garden."[7] Jonathan Edwards, who affirmed the existence of innate ideas, met the attack on them by revitalizing predestinarian theory and demonstrating its logical consistency with the psychological theories of his day. But Crèvecoeur believed in the shaping influence of environment and thus in the benign relationship between nature and human nature that made the life of the farmer a model of earthly felicity. He had, therefore, "to seal the garden" against both primitive savagery and civilized vice.

Clearly, James could not seal it when the Revolution occurred, and although Crèvecoeur through him asserts the possibility of doing so after the war, the evidence he himself provides predicts another outcome. If America is the land in which a farmer is so elevated by his position in the garden that he not only lives his happy condition but writes about it, then he participates in the very world he would keep at bay. The circumstance he does not perceive is that the world from which he wishes to remain immune is one that cooperates with his wish only so long as he is content to express himself in labor and leave representation in most of its principal functions—commercial, political, literary—to those who specialize in it. When James presumes to "letter it" with Mr. F. B. he unconsciously dismantles the order he celebrates.

The literary culture that was symbolized by a writing farmer was, to be sure, an idealization. Crèvecoeur, the actual author, was not a simple husbandman, and the flock of writings in the revolutionary period that were signed with such names as "Arator" or "Farmer" were not concerned with farming, the pen names being transparent devices whereby professional men, principally lawyers, claimed that they were speaking on behalf of plain people. The leaders who gathered at Philadelphia in the congress that yielded the Declaration of Independence hesitated over the issue of whether they, the people's representatives, had the authority to take a step not specifically authorized by the people; whether, that is, they, educated gentry, could speak as if they were indeed the farm folk of America, or whether they should recognize they were, in the main, lawyers, and so await a clearer voice from such folk before proceeding.[8] After some debate, they decided it was their duty to lead the folk while speaking for them. Their step proceeded in some part from an elitist assumption that the better-educated and wealthier segment should speak for the whole of society. But in greater part it proceeded from their sharing the culture embodied in Crèvecoeur's *Letters,* which encouraged them to believe that in America the gap between statesmen and farmers was not a significant one so that they could legitimately speak as their countrymen would.

American literary culture at the close of the eighteenth century was dominated by a relatively small group of professional men, principally ministers and lawyers, but while the term *elite* is often applied today to this group, it should be recognized that their elitism was qualified by their sense of the authority that resided in the people. This, as Edwards and Crèvecoeur revealed in their different ways, was a cultural condition before it was proclaimed as a political principle, which is to say that literature together with civil institutions such as church and family embodied the conditions of revolution before they were abstracted into political creeds and then embodied in political institutions. The authoring as well as the reading of texts was, as the writing farmer signaled, spreading beyond the learned class that had previously monopolized literature in America. Insofar as this class had addressed readers outside its ranks, it had treated them as passive recipients of their betters' wisdom, beneficiaries of instruction from ministers, statesmen, and scholars. But as printing presses multiplied in number and broke free from their concentration in a handful of population centers and were established in towns and villages, control of the text passed from author to reader. Retail sales increasingly replaced other forms of patronage, and a new readership in search of useful knowledge and rewarding amusement actively engaged texts, presuming to judge whether they were worthwhile and thus wresting interpretation from the authors.

Letters from an American Farmer embodies a culture at the turning point: written by a farmer yet still requiring the patronage of a great man; glorifying a natural harmony yet still depending upon imperial politics for its maintenance; asserting the ability of the yeoman to express his life yet still deploring the incursion of the represented into the world of the real. Its charm and energy derive from the coherence of a viewpoint so situated between new world and old with the middle ground of rural felicity that is its subject.

At the end, the Revolution having erupted to erase the middle, James views himself in the imagery of ruins: "I resemble, methinks, one of the stones of a ruined arch, still retaining that pristine form which anciently fitted the place I occupied, but the centre is tumbled down." But if his assuming the role of a writing farmer implicated him in the causes of the Revolution and so in what he for a moment perceives as ruin, the idea of nature he called upon to sanction his writing also sees him through the disruptions. The architectural image of ruins he invokes quickly gives place to a reliance upon the revitalizing force of nature, and he views his coming life among the Indians as "sufficiently complete to answer all the primary wants of man and to constitute him a social being such as he ought to be in the great forest of Nature" (p. 211).

There were no architectural ruins on the American landscape, and neither, finally, was there an idea of ruin in the culture.

CHAPTER THREE

REALIZING THE LANDSCAPE

European Rage for Ruins—American Natural History—Bartram's *Travels*—
Ordering the Exotic—Botanizing and Republicanism

O
N a sunny day in September 1786, soon after entering Italy on a journey he had long anticipated, Goethe paused in the town of Malesine in order to draw an old tower and adjoining walls that impressed him with the attractiveness of their decay. Despite the deterioration, however, the townspeople regarded their tower and walls as fortification, and suspecting the German stranger was a spy they summoned their podesta to look into the matter. When challenged, Goethe reported, he told the podesta, "I did not look upon that wall as a fortification. I called the attention of him and the people to the decay of the tower and walls, and to the generally defenceless position of the place, assuring him that I thought I only saw and drew a ruin." But, the townspeople asked, "If it was only a ruin, what could there be remarkable about it?" In answer, Goethe lectured the residents at length, explaining that not only classical antiquities but those of the Middle Ages deserved attention. Since they had grown up amidst these ruins, they failed to see how picturesque they were, he said, and he then went on to detail the beauties of the site. The distrustful townspeople stood before Goethe in order to keep an eye on him while he faced the wall. The situation obliged them constantly to

swivel their heads as he pointed out the successive details of interest in their ruins. "This scene appeared to me so ridiculous," he recorded, "that my good humour increased, and I spared them nothing—least of all the ivy, which had been suffered for ages to adorn the rocks and walls."[1]

Unknown to the citizens of Malesine, the rage for ruins was in full swing among the literati of Europe. Stimulated powerfully by the excavations at Herculaneum and Pompeii and Johann Winckelmann's enormously influential, illustrated masterpiece on ancient art, published in 1764, the craze, as Goethe was illustrating, had spread to medieval remains which were of interest precisely because they were in ruin.

In the England of Crèvecoeur's assumed correspondent, F. B., who had himself visited Pompeii, wealthy persons were arranging for the construction on their estates of brand-new ruins, crumbling towers and decaying walls built to order. "A piece of Palladian architecture may be elegant in the last degree," the landscape architect William Gilpin wrote in 1794, but it lacks picturesque beauty. To attain this "we must beat down half of it, deface the other, and throw the mutilated members around in heaps. In short, from a *smooth* building we must turn it into a *rough* ruin." And he went on to suggest the same procedure with the landscape: "Make it *rough* and you make it *picturesque*."[2]

Such an aesthetic had a literary dimension, embodied, for example, in *The Pleasures of Melancholy* (1745), a poem by the young Oxonian, Thomas Warton, in which melancholy as contrasted with mirth is affirmed to be the condition of genuine sensibility.[3] Its pleasures come to those who have the philosophical disposition to perceive the transitory nature of human achievements and, accordingly, to live a life of sensitive awareness of the inevitable wreck of mortal things. In Warton's poem, a hermit contemplating the ruins of Persepolis is shown to be superior in feeling to a shepherd dazzled by a glittering glimpse of Athens, while Cosmelia, the figure of mirth, is exposed as contemptibly trivial in her pursuit of pleasures in the world of London fashion. Melancholy affords the deeper pleasure, exempt from change because it comprehends it through contemplation rather than opposes it through action. Ruins were object lessons in the vanity of human ambition, and the rage for them reinforced both social and political conservatism.

With its notable lack of ruins, the American scene was all too clearly an antiaesthetic one, and, by the same token, a politically progressive one. Musing on an Indian burial ground, for example, Chateaubriand recognized its aesthetic shortcomings when compared with European graveyards, but, committed as he was to progress, he found the American vacancy an ideal arena for the nurturing of the liberty which could eventually become the essence of societies everywhere.[4] And, indeed, with aesthetic conventions so firmly fixed on landscapes that contained the lessons of ruins, the writers who wished to describe America were compelled from the present into the future tense. The absence of ruins argued the presence of promise, and the writer's task was to read the landscape as the site of a happier society than had ever before existed.

When Farmer James's minister urged him to write his letters, he had to overcome not only James's feelings of inadequacy as a penman but his sense that in conventional terms America gave him nothing to write about. The minister argued:

> I am sure I cannot be called a partial American when I say that the spectacle afforded by these pleasing scenes may be more entertaining and more philosophical than that which arises from beholding the musty ruins of Rome. Here everything would inspire the reflecting traveller with the most philanthropic ideas; his imagination instead of submitting to the painful and useless retrospect of revolutions, desolations, and plagues, would, on the contrary, wisely spring forward to the anticipated fields of future cultivation and improvement, to the future extent of those generations which are to replenish and embellish this boundless continent. There the half-

ruined amphitheatres and the putrid fevers of the Campania must fill the mind with the most melancholy reflections whilst he is seeking for the origin and the intention of those structures with which he is surrounded and for the cause of so great a decay. Here he might contemplate the very beginnings and outlines of human society which can be traced nowhere but in this great part of the world.[5]

Accordingly, the novel task Crèvecoeur undertook was a travelogue across a relatively featureless present where primitive nature was read as an encouragement to human endeavor rather than a description of a monument-strewn present where ruins were read as signs of human limitation. It demanded that the observer reason from rude appearances to their social value rather than contemplate lessons written in fragments. His concern was with the possibility of achieving a happy and thriving society through the purposeful development of a cooperating natural scene. The certainty of mortality was no barrier to the felicitous continuity of the generations if their society was justly founded on the principles of nature.

In his study of the forms of ruin in Romantic literature, Thomas McFarland observed that "the pervasive longing of the Romantic for an absent reality was at the same time an index to a prevailing sense of incompleteness, fragmentation, and ruin."[6] The fascination with ruins, that is, was the corollary of a yearning for a lost wholeness. In America, we observe, the matter was opposite. Crèvecoeur and others saw the reality of wholeness as incipient in a landscape awaiting the labor of reasonable men for its fruition. The lesson of ruins did not reside in the observation that all things decay. Ruins taught the avoidance of the aggrandizement of property and power that had led to the wasting away of old-world civilizations. History in the new world could be progressive rather than tied to the cycle of rise and fall.

Schiller said his age was afflicted by a sense of fragmentation because "as soon as enlarged experience and more precise speculation made necessary a sharp division of the sciences, on the one hand, and on the other, the more intricate dissociation of ranks and occupations, the essential bond of human nature was torn apart."[7] Conversely, the American perception of wholeness rather than fragmentation grew from a society that was essentially free of the everyday consequentiality of articulations of rank, although, as we have observed, Crèvecoeur unconsciously undermined his thesis when he attempted to overcome the dissociation of farming from writing. But his theme is wholeness, and his Pennsylvania farm is not just a part of America but a synecdoche for the whole that can come into being.

Schiller also cited the sharper division of the sciences that grew from enlarged experience and more precise speculation as contributing to the strong European sense of fragmentation. This too was controverted in American discourse. Indeed, modern science, more particularly natural history, was seen to provide the system whereby the world could be perceived and ordered into the whole it was. Thomas Jefferson, for example, assiduously studied the natural history of his native region in search of clues both to its prehistoric past and its future development. In his *Notes on Virginia* (written 1781–82) he sought to refute Buffon's notorious contention that all species in America were naturally smaller than their European counterparts, and when in the endeavor he strayed from sound scientific reason, as, for example, in his argument that the mammoth must still be extant in North America, he did so on the basis of the proposition that "such is the economy of nature, that no instance can be produced of her having permitted any one race of her animals to become extinct; of her having formed any link in her great work so weak as to be broken."[8] His statement proceeded from so great a conviction of the perfect wholeness of the natural world that it would admit neither anomaly nor extinction. Even with regard to species, there were no ruins in America.

Fresh from his travels through France and Italy, in June 1788

Jefferson supplied American friends with notes to guide their own travels in Europe, emphasizing that he ordered them in terms of what was useful for them as Americans. It is not surprising that agriculture, practical mechanics, and gardens head the list of the kinds of things to be observed. When architecture, a particular passion of his, is mentioned, Jefferson notes that "as we double our numbers every twenty years we must double our houses." Architecture is, then, a vital art for Americans "and it is desirable to introduce taste into an art which shows so much." He lists painting and statuary as "worth seeing but not studying." Ruins and monuments, however, he does not list at all.[9]

European literati touring America, on the other hand, were guided by Crèvecoeur's work and by the *Travels* of William Bartram. So indebted was Chateaubriand to the latter work that in his account of his own travels he reproduced large extracts from it, saying that he had so assimilated Bartram's work "that it is almost impossible for me to separate what is mine from what is Bartram's, or indeed frequently even to recognize it."[10]

The eleventh of Crèvecoeur's twelve letters is devoted to a description of William's father, John Bartram, his farm, and his work on the banks of the Schuylkill River near Philadelphia. As an unbookish and sparsely educated Quaker lad, the elder Bartram had early been so attracted to the study of plants that his growing interest in the subject led him to hire a tutor to teach him the Latin he needed to be able to read Linnaeus. His studies impelled him into annual journeys to other colonies for gathering specimens and he conducted early, perhaps the earliest, American experiments in hybridization. He entered into correspondence with European botanists, most notably Linnaeus himself, who sent his disciple, Peter Kalm, from Sweden to visit Bartram. Kalm praised Bartram's judgment and his "attention which lets nothing escape unnoticed," and he regretted that Bartram was so negligent a penman that he failed to write down all his numerous and useful observations.[11] Linnaeus

said he regarded Bartram as the greatest "natural botanist" of his
day.

Another correspondent was the eminent Quaker man of science
in London, Peter Collinson, who was also the recipient of Benjamin
Franklin's scientific communications, most notably those on electricity. The Quaker connection served to link eminent Philadelphians
with the Royal Society even when, as in Bartram's case, the Quaker
had turned heterodox, or, as in Franklin's, the correspondent was
but a friend of the Friends. Whatever Quakerism subtracted from
the recreation of the mind because of its distrust of art and display
was, it seems, replaced by a devotion to the study of the creation
as a recreation. Collinson procured Bartram's appointment, at fifty
pounds a year, as Royal Botanist to George III, and Bartram also
supplied specimens and information to other royal courts and other
European men of science. His eminence was a source of American
pride, and he was featured together with such as Washington, David
Rittenhouse (practical astronomer), Thomas Godfrey (inventor of
a highly improved quadrant), and Franklin in lists drawn up to
demonstrate that genius flourished as well in the new world as it
did in the old.

Benjamin Franklin offered a characteristically American estimate
of the value of Bartram's work measured against that of travel writers
on Europe when he wrote in 1769 to encourage him to publish his
observations "and point out the Advantages that may be drawn from
the Whole, in publick Undertakings or particular private Practice.
It is true many People are fond of old Buildings, Monuments, &c.
but there is a Number which would be much better pleas'd with
such Accounts as you could afford them: And for one I confess that
if I could find in any Italian Travels a Receipt for making Parmesan
Cheese, it would give me more Satisfaction than a Transcription of
any Inscription from any old Stone whatever."[12]

John Bartram's son William was born on the family farm in 1733
and early showed a talent for drawing. Franklin offered to teach

him the printing trade, believing he had a special aptitude for engraving, but William first attempted to gain his living as an independent trader at Cape Fear, North Carolina. Unsuccessful at this, he was next attracted to the possibility of becoming a planter on the St. John's River in Florida, a region he had explored in 1765–66 when he accompanied his father on a botanizing expedition. But this too came to nothing and in the following year he was back home.

Meanwhile, Peter Collinson had shown William's drawings to another London Friend and botanist, Dr. John Fothergill, who on their strength agreed to meet the expenses of another journey William would make to the southeast in exchange for seeds and specimens to be sent to him. William Bartram made that long journey of exploration in 1773–77, but whether because of the disruption in relations between England and the colonies or his own negligence, he supplied very little of what Fothergill had been expecting. He did, however, provide the world with far more than any one had anticipated: a book that came to be regarded as a minor masterpiece of English prose, a major work of American literature—still in print today and still a pleasure to read—and, to the eye of many a sensitive reader, Wordsworth and Coleridge among them, a marvelous treasury of American exotica. Carlyle, indeed, told Emerson that the work should be regarded as an American bible.

The full title of Bartram's book is *Travels through North and South Carolina, Georgia, East and West Florida, the Cherokee Country, the Extensive Territories of the Muscogulges, or Creek Confederacy, and the Country of the Chactaws.* Published in Philadelphia in 1791, it was soon republished there and in London and Dublin. Within the decade it was translated into German, Dutch, and French.

The work has two focuses. The major one is the description of fauna as well as flora, description that calls new natural phenomena into existence through lively and often surprisingly lush verbal accounts of flower, fish, or animal in its natural setting—nothing is described disconnected from its surroundings—together with a studied application of Latin names to each in accordance with the Linnaean system so that, at the same time, it is lifted from its environment and fixed into the universal order of things.

The second focus, to which, roughly, one fourth of the book is devoted, is a characterization of the Indian tribes of the Florida region. Again descriptive prose that renders them in their setting is accompanied by a cataloguing, not, to be sure, with Latin names, but still a cataloguing of Indian towns and tongues that orders them objectively.

For all his fascination with the world before his eyes, Bartram unhesitatingly claims his reader's attention to its details not so much for what they are in themselves as for the ways in which they can be seen to fulfill the end for which they exist, the serving of mankind. "Whatever may contribute to our existence is . . . of importance," he insists, "whether it be found in the animal or vegetable kingdom."[13] And embracing the myriad of his observations is his sense that they culminate in God. After naming a number of plants, for example, he writes, "Though none of these most useful tribes are conspicuous for stateliness, figure, or splendour, yet their valuable qualities and virtues excite love, gratitude, and adoration to the great Creator, who was pleased to endow them with such eminent qualities, and to reveal them to us for our sustenance, amusement, and delight" (*Travels*, p. 17).

Bartram affords ample amusement and delight in his accounts of alligators, bears, and flesh-eating plants, but always at the fore is the value conveyed by such terms as "useful" and "sustenance." Worship may be the final cause of creation, but its formal cause is human need. Like Crèvecoeur, Chateaubriand, Jefferson, and other depicters of American nature, Bartram regards the landscape as the womb of a wonderful future rather than the burial place of a monitory past.

A striking illustration occurs when Bartram visits Silver Bluff in

Georgia, "a pleasant villa, the property and seat of C. Golphin," a trader with extensive connections among the Indian tribes of the region. As Bartram wanders in the vicinity, he finds

> various monuments and vestiges of the residence of the ancients; as Indian conical mounts, terraces, areas, &c. as well as remains or traces of fortresses of regular formation, as if constructed after the modes of European military architects, which are supposed to be ancient camps of the Spaniards who formerly fixed themselves at this place in hope of finding silver.
>
> But perhaps Mr. Golphin's buildings and improvements will prove to be the foundation of monuments of infinitely greater celebrity and permanency than either of the preceding establishments. (pp. 258–59)

The passage epitomizes the progressivist antiaesthetic of a great deal of the day's American discourse. Civilizations of the past as represented by the ancient Indian and sixteenth-century Spanish remains, the conical mounts and the traces of fortification, do not engage his imagination as do the plants he discusses at length elsewhere in his account. Nor do they lead him to reflect on the inescapability of decay. Instead he turns to Golphin's "improvements" and expresses a belief that the permanence that escaped native agriculturists and foreign treasure seekers can be secured by modern traders.

Armed with the Linnaean system, Bartram traversed an exotic landscape with the certainty that each part of it could be classified so as to indicate not only its participation in a whole but its similarity to all other parts of that whole. The world of nature was not marked by strong divisions nor did it admit of lacunae but was ordered into groups (Bartram was fond of applying the anthropomorphic terminology of tribes and families to plants and animals) that reflected one another: plants were similar to oviparous animals; oviparous to viviparous animals; viviparous animals to man. Even so apparent an anomaly as a flesh-eating plant had its place. The whole went on as smoothly as an ideal machine because, for Bartram, that was precisely what it was, a mechanism made up of an infinity of mechanisms, each regulated in relation to the others and the whole animated by God the maker.

As Garry Wills has reminded us, prior to the romantic reaction against the Industrial Revolution, the vision of animate life as a machine was a liberating one.[14] In proclaiming the perfection of the universal machine, Bartram was ennobling its most splendid part, the human machine, with which all other mechanisms were designed to mesh.

So strongly does imminent wholeness impress itself upon Bartram that at times he appears incapable of seeing only the part present before his eyes. Consider, for example, the following passage. His manifest intent is to provide a description of *Pistia stratiotes,* sea lettuce, but his imagination moves his vision from this description to a fuller scene than he actually views, as if the part so strongly means the whole that the whole is already there. The plant, Bartram writes,

> vegetates on the surface of the still stagnant water; and in its natural situation, is propagated from seed only. In great storms of wind and rain, when the river is suddenly raised, large masses of these floating plants are broken loose, and driven from the shores, into the wide water, where they have the appearance of islets, and float about, until broken to pieces by the wind and waves; or driven again to shore, on some distant coast of the river, where they again find footing, and there forming new colonies, spread and extend themselves again, until again broken up and dispersed as before. These floating islands present a very entertaining prospect: for although we behold an assemblage of the primary productions of nature only, yet the imagination seems to remain in suspense and doubt; as in order to enliven the delusion and form a most picturesque appearance, we see not only flowery plants, clumps of shrubs,

old weather-beaten trees, hoary and barbed, with the long moss waving from their snags, but we also see them completely inhabited, and alive, with crocodiles, serpents, frogs, otters, crows, herons, curlews, jackdaws, &c. There seems, in short, nothing wanted but the appearance of a wigwam and a canoe to complete the scene. (*Travels,* pp. 93–94)

As for the European observer of ruins the story of a past civilization inheres in the falling tower, so for Bartram the entire economy of life inheres in a rank plant growing in stale water. The imagination adds birds and beasts and longs further to add the signs of human presence. But whereas the picturesqueness of the tower is shadowed by an awareness of death, the picturesqueness of the islet of sea lettuce is animated by the multiplication of life. Missing from Bartram's perception is any sense of irony implicit in man's attempts to defeat mortality by leaving his mark on the landscape. His activity, rather, comes as a fulfillment of that landscape.

For a brief period during the early part of his travels in eastern Florida, Bartram was accompanied by "a young mechanic on his adventures," who "seemed to be actuated by no other motive, than either to establish himself in some well-inhabited part of the country, where, by following his occupation, he might be enabled to procure, without much toil and danger, the necessaries and conveniences of life; or by industry and frugality, perhaps establish his fortune." His own motives, Bartram says, are different, stemming as they do from a curiosity about the productions of nature and a desire to make discoveries. But the most striking aspect of Bartram's comparison of himself with the young mechanic whose views were "probably totally opposite" is that he suggested that "each of our pursuits was perhaps equally laudable." Although the mechanic sought a society in which to establish himself while Bartram's path led him farther into less settled regions, still Bartram hoped to introduce his native country to "some original productions of nature, which might be-

come useful to society" (p. 82). He is constantly aware of his connection with society and its connection to the nature he explores.
Unlike the later, more romantic celebrators of the wild, he does not
require a contrasting critique of the city to highlight the values he
finds in nature but esteems them for what they can contribute to
society.

When he addresses Indian life, Bartram continues to deny difference. He starts to praise the virtue of "the untutored savages,"
but brings himself up short, realizing that such praise is trite. Moreover, as he ponders the matter that phrase strikes him as the reverse
of truth because once he begins residence among them it becomes
clear to him that they are "both well-tutored and civil" (p. 111).
The Indians, that is, are like other men not only biologically but in
their social habits. And as for their notoriously bellicose behavior,
it is no different from that of other nations, proceeding from the
same motives that lead to the exercise of arms among civilized
peoples. The Muscogulges do not wage war from a "capricious
desire of shedding blood," nor do they do so from an avarice for
plunder. Rather, they fight the neighboring tribes in order to unite
"all nations and languages under one universal confederacy or commonwealth" (pp. 315–16). This, Bartram affirms, is a magnanimous
intention based on principle. When they exercise their desire to
obliterate differences, albeit by force, they are offering positive proof
of their social instincts and their awareness that all parts of the
creation tend toward coherence.

When Bartram cites the drive toward confederation as a justi-
fiable reason for Indian warfare, it is tempting to see this as an
appeal to the sympathy of his countrymen who were themselves in
the process of war and confederation. But this allusion is questionable. The *Travels,* like Crèvecoeur's *Letters,* is, in the main, the work
of a British colonist, and the advent of the Revolution has no explicit
bearing on his subject matter, which is a description of the natural
phenomena of the southeastern region and an account of their social

usefulness. Insofar as Bartram organizes his work along the spine of his travels—and the narrative account so frequently pauses for extended descriptions that it is not dominant—those travels end when he crosses the Susquehanna into Lancaster on the ice, "and in two days more arrived at my father's house on the banks of the river Schuylkill, within four miles of the city, January 1778" (p. 379). By then, Burgoyne had been defeated at Saratoga, France had decided to recognize the independence of the states, and the Articles of Confederation had been adopted by Congress. But no mention of war or politics is made as he recounts the itinerary of his reentry into the rebelling colonies.

If our concern, however, is with the reality constituted by the text rather than with its reflection of public events external to it, then Bartram's *Travels* tells us something about an American state of mind that is characteristic of the literary culture which, in turn, connects with public events. Most obviously, although Americans quickly came to see that their struggle had large historical consequences, they did so from a frame of reference outside history. The absence of ruins argued for an American history undetermined by the past, a history that could actually begin at the beginning. After closing his narrative with his return home, Bartram appended as part of his book his account of the persons, manners, customs, and government of the Muscogulge Confederacy, and the very last words of his book acknowledge the traces of the past only to dismiss their importance: "To conclude this subject concerning the monuments of the Americans"—a noteworthy application of the term to the native population, not the colonists—"I deem it necessary to observe, as my opinion, that none of them I have seen discover the least signs of the arts, sciences, or architectures of the Europeans or other inhabitants of the old world; yet evidently betray every sign or marks of the most distant antiquity" (p. 408). Unlike the America of Edwards, one that was newly discovered in order to fulfill the already written history of redemption, this America exists independent of the rest

of the world, its ancient monuments prompting no conclusion other
than that time is yet to begin there.

In a modern study of travel literature, Wayne Franklin speaks
of "the simplest and most delightful variety of the New World travel
books," which "tends whenever possible to rely on a group of
presentational means in which time plays no crucial role—catalogs,
tables, descriptions, discourses, expositions—forms which by their
own static, even iconographic nature convey writer and reader alike
into a state of existence beyond the limits and confusions of a historical moment."[15] The point applies to Bartram's *Travels,* in which
animated descriptions mingle with categorized lists and the exotic
phenomena of the Florida region are rendered in all their lushness
and yet tagged with Latin names that lift them out of their environment. The state of existence thus presented is, indeed, beyond
historical moment, but, of course, this sense of a realm as yet unaffected by history is historically specific.

At one remarkable point in the *Travels,* Bartram's concern with
presentation emerges as subject matter as well as method. He is
engaged in his customary task of describing a scene to readers who
have never viewed the like, but so extraordinary is this particular
sight that he is moved to comment on the relation of what appears
before his eye, and thus what he reports to us, to what that appearance really means; moved, that is, to question whether appearances in nature may not conceal the truth of what is pictured rather
than signify it. On the Alachua Savanna six miles above Lake George
in Florida, Bartram comes across a great sink or basin of water and
seats himself on a "swelling green knoll" between, on his right, an
orange grove interspersed with palms and magnolias, and, on his
left, a grove of the aromatic Illium Floridanum. Before him lies the
water.

> Behold . . . a vast circular expanse before you, the waters of
> which are so extremely clear as to be absolutely diaphanous or

transparent as the ether; the margin of the bason ornamented with a great variety of fruitful and floriferous trees, shrubs, and plants, the pendant golden Orange dancing on the surface of the pellucid waters, the balmy air vibrating with the melody of the merry birds, tenants of the encircling aromatic grove.

At the same instant innumerable bands of fish are seen, some clothed in the most brilliant colours; the voracious crocodile stretched along at full length, as the great trunk of a tree in size; the devouring garfish, inimical trout, and all the varieties of gilded painted bream; the barbed catfish, dreaded sting-ray, skate, and flounder, spotted bass, sheeps head and ominous drum; all in their separate bands and communities, with free and unsuspicious intercourse performing their evolutions: there are no signs of enmity, no attempt to devour each other; the different bands seem peacably and complaisantly to move a little aside, as it were to make room for others to pass by.

But behold yet something far more admirable, see whole armies descending into an abyss, the mouth of the bubbling fountain: they disappear! are they gone for ever? I raise my eye with terror and astonishment; I look down again to the fountain with anxiety, when behold them as it were emerging from the blue ether of another world, apparently at a vast distance; at their first appearance no bigger than flies or minnows; now gradually enlarging, their brilliant colours begin to paint the fluid.

Now they come forward rapidly, and instantly emerge, with the elastic expanding column of crystalline waters, into the circular bason or funnel: see how gently they rise, some upright, others obliquely, or seem to lie as it were on their sides, suffering themselves to be gently lifted or bourne up by the expanding fluid towards the surface, sailing or floating like butterflies in the cerulean ether: then again they as gently descend, diverge and move off; when they rally, form again, and rejoin their kindred tribes.

This amazing and delightful scene, though real, appears at first but as a piece of excellent painting; there seems no medium; you imagine the picture to be within a few inches of your eyes, and that you may without the least difficulty touch any one of the fish, or put your finger upon the crocodile's eye, when it really is twenty or thirty feet under water.

And although this paradise of fish may seem to exhibit a just representation of the peaceable and happy state of nature which existed before the fall, yet in reality it is a mere representation; for the nature of the fish is the same as if they were in Lake George or the river; but here the water or element in which they live and move, is so perfectly clear and transparent, it places them all on an equality with regard to their ability to injure or escape from one another; (as all river fish of prey, or such as feed upon each other, as well as the unwieldy crocodile, take their prey by surprising; secreting themselves under covert or in ambush, until an opportunity offers, when they rush suddenly upon them:) but here is no covert, no ambush; here the trout freely passes by the very nose of the alligator, and laughs in his face, and the bream by the trout.

But what is really surprising is, that the consciousness of each other's safety, or some other latent cause, should so absolutely alter their conduct, for here is not the least attempt made to injure or disturb one another. (pp. 150–51)

This remarkable passage coheres into a picture that seems to insist upon being read as an emblem. Initially, it appears to stand as a natural equivalent of the painted peaceable kingdom in which the lion lies down with the lamb. But unlike the painting, it is not a realm of perfection that will arrive when history ends but part of the everyday creation we inhabit. There before Bartram's eyes the denizens of the basin constantly move from their variegated activity to annihilation in the monochromatic source only to reemerge and again color the world with their activity. The scene appears to symbolize a state of existence actually accessible in America rather than one that must await the afterlife.

Bartram explicitly cautions against our indulgence in such a reading. But the very circumstance that leads him to warn us can be cited to further that reading. The medium in which the fish move, he reminds us, is abnormally clear, and this deprives them of the cover necessary for the pursuit of their predatory instincts. Their nature, he asserts, is unchanged. But, we note, their behavior is changed because their environment is clarified, which leads us to conjecture that even if a modified environment cannot alter nature it can alter social conduct. This being so, the possibility of behavior becoming second nature calls into question the ultimate importance of primary nature. The difference between appearance and reality in social conduct may continue to remain a matter of ontological moment but it loses its practical importance. So long as we retain a clear view of how others behave we may take this as the reality; it is the truth about them so far as they concern us. A society with relatively few class barriers and a natural setting of abundant resources combined to form the cultural belief that human nature was as malleable as the landscape. It could be perfected in a social environment that rewarded behavior that contributed to the harmony of the whole, and inhibited, if it did not eliminate, unearned privileges or any other source of authority that presumed to be above public accountability; an environment, in short, free of the social equivalents of the ambush that permits large fish to prey on smaller. Print, making the private public and affording no hiding place for vice is, then, the crucial medium of such a society.[16]

Bartram's basin can be read as a representation of a perceived if unarticulated social condition. Although he was a natural historian, his work is not so distinct from that of the social historian as later, more "scientific" natural history would be, as his persistent dedication to the useful indicates. His method and his content combine to constitute a perception of reality that extends beyond his manifest project of describing and classifying.

Michel Foucault observes that "the deferred but insistent unity of a *Taxonomia universalis* appeared in all clarity in the work of Linnaeus when he conceived the project of discovering in all the concrete domains of nature or society the same distribution and the same order."[17] Bartram was an avid apostle of this project and America the theater for its demonstration. In America, moreover, the Linnaean system appeared to break down previous social as well as natural boundaries since its laboratory was the field and wood available to all who made the preliminary effort of learning the language of taxonomy. This was the ground for the realization of James's fictional relationship with F. B., and for the actual correspondence of Bartram with Fothergill and his father with royal courts. In 1803 Samuel Miller of New York surveyed the century just past in his country and said of Linnaeus: "He formed a language so simple and luminous, and so adjusted by its several parts to his improved doctrine, that the acquisition of botany became a far more easy task than before. In fact, this was so much the case, that instead of remaining an abstruse study, confined to the schools, as formerly, it was converted into an agreeable amusement, to persons of leisure in all ranks and situations."[18] Eighteenth-century science and republican America seemed linked in mutual validation while both continued to be vexed by the imperfections of representation. The slippage Bartram felt in going from the natural world to its representation is analogous to the political slippage that occurred in going from the body of society to its representation in a republican assembly. But in both spheres the nature of authority was broadening.

Widespread interest in natural history, and botany in particular, functioned as a new-world opposite to the old-world rage for ruins: it was taken up not just by the wealthy but by people in all walks of life; it did not require travel to special sites but could be pursued in one's immediate vicinity; it was unconcerned with the past, but, focusing on the organic, was concerned with the present and the future it contained.

This view of botanizing America requires, to be sure, some qualification. A canvasser sent out from Philadelphia to find subscribers for a botany book, for example, reported back to the home office in some exasperation. His letter from Baltimore, dated October 10, 1817, told Mathew Carey:

You may in mind assimilate my business to water running down hill, but let me tell you it would be more just if you compared it to a shad climbing a pine tree.

In the first place there isn't more than 1 to 500 who knows what Botany is, that is, one you've to search for (once in 3 mos. you may find him *unengaged* at home) then you have to convince him of an *American* production of the kind (for many possess extensive histories of exotic plants), after put down his prejudices against subscription & at last wait the will and pleasure of the *whole* family (when composed of girls more easy) and should success attend you, in verity Pat git one whole *subscriber!*[19]

Although it serves to qualify generalizations about botanizing America, the letter's emphasis on the limited market for a botany book must also be read as determined by the particular situation of a salesman anxious to justify his record. What stands forth vividly, nonetheless, is that the readership for such a book was visualized as the family, not the individual, with the female at least as prominent as the male reader. The assumption of such a readership reinforces the idea of a culture oriented toward the future and essentially indifferent to notions of the pleasures of melancholy, which are both backward gazing and indulged in solitude.

CHAPTER FOUR

GAINING CONFIDENCE

Identity and Duplicity—Stephen Burroughs and Confidence—*Charlotte Temple* and Real Property—*Arthur Mervyn* and Personal Property

ROTESTANT tradition located identity in the soul. The relationship of an individual to other individuals as manifested in behavior was a matter of appearance, while reality resided in an inner condition invisible to all but the deity. To be sure, negative signs such as licentious behavior or the profession of heretical opinions were fairly reliable indices of a depraved soul, but their reverse, moral conduct and the profession of orthodox belief, were, it was recognized, not entirely reliable indications of a saved condition. Piety would necessarily result in morality, but morality could be simulated for worldly ends and was not thus a sure sign of piety. The reality that counted was internal, not a matter of appearance.

In a society such as Puritan New England, which rewarded acknowledged believers with civic and economic privileges, the temptation to feign the signs of salvation was great, and, it was assumed, some did so successfully in the visible world. Accordingly, Protestant culture was acutely sensitive to its vulnerability to hypocrisy. Spenser's arch villain, Archimago, is the master of hypocrisy; Milton's Satan succeeds in entering paradise because not even angels can detect hypocrisy.

By the middle decades of the eighteenth century, however, emphasis had shifted, and increasingly in Protestant America social conduct was taken as an adequate sign of individual virtue and individual virtue, in turn, taken as an adequate sign of the sanctity of the soul. Independence, republican government, and the volatile range of economic opportunities in the new nation accelerated the process that led one political and religious conservative to the following observation at the time of Jefferson's presidency:

> In established society, influence is chiefly the result of personal character, seen and known through the period in which the character is formed and the conduct by which it is displayed. In such society, notwithstanding the corruption of the present world, a man of worth and wisdom will, unless prevented by particular circumstances, be almost always more respectfully regarded than persons destitute of these characteristics, and will have a superior efficacy in the affairs of those around him. But in a state of society recently begun, influence is chiefly gained by those who directly seek it; and these in almost all instances are the ardent and bustling. Such men make bold pretensions to qualities which they do not possess, clamor everywhere about liberty and rights, are patriots of course, and jealous of the encroachments of those in power, thrum over incessantly the importance of public economy, stigmatize every just and honorable public expenditure, arraign the integrity of those whose wisdom is undisputed, and the wisdom of those whose integrity cannot be questioned, and profess universally the very principles and feelings of him with whom they are conversing.[1]

In "established society" persons were known over a period of years, but in the new society in which upward social mobility was frequently pursued through movement into growing cities or onto new lands, persons were known principally by what they represented themselves as being. Whatever its theological import, hypocrisy was no longer a grave social concern. By the same token, with conduct no longer grounded in grace and personality no longer "seen and known through the period in which the character is formed and the conduct by which it is displayed," vulnerability to duplicity became a consuming social concern. Almost every novel or personal narrative in English written from the mid-eighteenth through the early nineteenth century has at least one major episode of deception, confidence misplaced in a seeming friend, and many make such deceptions the dominant theme. Archimago and Satan who preyed on souls were replaced by the human deceivers who preyed on the property of men and the chastity of women.

The period's most popular literary entertainment, the novel of seduction, strikingly embodies society's pervasive suspicion that deceit is latent in every relationship. The novel throve on the theme of the fatal consequences of seduction while, in point of fact, seduction itself posed little threat in an America in which there was a steady rise in premarital intercourse from the beginning of the eighteenth century to a peak at around 1800 when as many as one in every three brides was pregnant at the time of her marriage. As the historian James Henratta has pointed out, "this alteration in sexual behavior did not endanger the traditional nuclear family (since conception was followed by marriage and not by illegitimate birth)."[2] The popularity of the novel of seduction in America does not, then, stem from the applicability of its explicit message. Beneath its detailing of the threat to traditional standards of female conduct another concern was at stake, one for which sexual misconduct served as an attractive dramatic vehicle. This was a concern with the destructive consequences of a discrepancy between what another represented himself as and the self he truly was, an anxiety about the ease with which persons could be separated from property in a mobile society in which traditional guides to an individual's worth were unavailable or inapplicable so that self-representation had to be accepted as the self. Too often circumstances revealed a difference only after the damage had been done.

It is no accident that novels that centered upon the seduced and abandoned woman almost always also included at least one man, usually her father, who had been driven to financial ruin through signing a note for a false friend. Although peripheral to the main narrative and detachable from it in formal terms, the bankruptcy subplot sounded the theme of trust betrayed and social identity destroyed which was more fully enacted in the plot of sexual seduction. Additionally, of course, it underlined the message that chastity was negotiable property. The disaster that awaited the seduced maiden who failed to secure marriage in exchange for her virginity was paralleled by the ruin that awaited her father when he failed to secure collateral from the seeming friend for whom he signed a note.

Henry Fielding's Tom Jones left the West Country and journeyed to London across a landscape he had never before encountered. Time and again as strangers sought to estimate him they did so in terms of his obvious membership in an upper class, a condition about which they were not easily fooled since their entire lives—whether they were strumpets, publicans, or gentlefolk—had been shaped by their awareness of class, and their welfare was keyed to their ability to locate strangers in its terms. Moreover, far as he might have been from home, Tom was rarely in any community that had not heard of the family in which he was raised, and once this was known, he, as it were, was known.

In America, however, even before independence and markedly after it, such signs did not serve. While classes did exist, class structure did not play so defining a role. Upward social mobility was valued and its achievement was tied in good part to geographical mobility. The way up was to get out into an area long on resources and short on manpower. Although one did not necessarily leave home in order to escape being known, one usually did venture into a society in which family provided little clue to identity and where, if one wished, it was possible to invent background even as one attempted to create a foreground. Benjamin Franklin rose socially to stand before kings, and to do so he also ran away from his family to another province to live among those who had no way of measuring who he was save by how he represented himself. Charles Brockden Brown's fictional Arthur Mervyn, a lad from the country wandering in the city, is only who he says he is, and those who befriend and employ him accept him on these terms and then allow his behavior to speak for him.

Because of its chronic need for manpower as well as its attachment to the doctrine of equality, the society in which such figures moved permitted a stranger some initial acceptance into it on his own terms rather than those of family or class. Moreover, such self-representations, abstractions from the immanent selves known to all in a community where one had lived from birth, were paralleled by what was, in Henratta's words, "the increasing predominance of personal wealth (in the form of cash, mortgages, loans, and movable goods) over landed property."[3] We remember the young Franklin's commercial foothold in Philadelphia was secured by his collecting a note for a friend and using the capital for his own ends without authorization (albeit he eventually repaid the "borrowed" amount). Analogously, in Brown's novels, *Arthur Mervyn* (1799) and *Edgar Huntly* (1799), the dominant theme of the questionable reliability of self-representation is played out in plots that also contain seemingly superfluous episodes concerned with the wealth to be acquired from the mere cashing of a note by its possessor regardless of whose labor or property gave that note its monetary value.

To examine the theme of deceitful appearances in American writings of the turn of the century is, however, to discern that its powerful hold on the imagination does not stem simply from a dread of it, but from the mixture of that dread with a fascination at the capacity of appearance to convert itself into the truth of social reality. Representation—personal, commercial, political—could deceive in that it falsified what it purported to represent, but it could also be seen as not so much opposed to or measurable by an immanent world apart from it as it was constitutive of that world.

~~~velllQQJJnuan~~~

Memoirs of the Notorious Stephen Burroughs of New Hampshire was first published in 1798 and in the following years reappeared in numerous editions, some containing a supplement written by Burroughs and all containing annotations by one or another editor eager to point the moral lessons to be drawn from Burroughs's career. By 1900, thirty editions had been published in fourteen different cities. It was a popular book because by the time of the first edition Stephen Burroughs, although but thirty years old, was already a legendary figure, known in the villages of New England and New York through the many tales told of his escapades. In these accounts, Burroughs was a demonically assisted, criminally dangerous prankster who held nothing—family, religion, female chastity, property, social harmony—sacred, could be contained by no jail, and was so plausible a confidence man that he might, indeed, at that very moment be the clergyman or schoolmaster who had recently arrived in the district. As the legend spread, strangers apprehended for criminal deception in one or another town gave their names as Stephen Burroughs. He seemed not only duplicitous but ubiquitous. Since it was known that Stephen Burroughs would never acknowledge his identity, one of his impenetrable disguises may have been his claim that he was indeed Stephen Burroughs.

Clearly the lure of the growing canon of Burroughs stories stemmed from the unacknowledged attraction of his impieties. He was a one-man saturnalia whose reported adventures permitted his audience the satisfaction of vicarious participation in a rebellion against the constraints of the sexual code (the women Burroughs "seduced" did not appear to be unwilling), orthodox religion, and village autocracies. Understandably, therefore, alongside the story of a demonic Burroughs there grew up an account of a Robin Hood Burroughs who preyed only on the rich and pompous in order to benefit the poor and humble by redistributing the wealth and deflating the pretentious.

The *Memoirs* surpasses any fiction of the period in its rendering of the texture of eighteenth-century American village life with its bickerings, jealousies, prejudices, and, at rare moments, generosities and pleasures. Unlike the period's novels, Burroughs's work is localized in space and time and consistent with data available apart from it. His account of many of his activities may be fictionalized, but there is no reason to regard his work as less historical than other personal narratives of the period such as those by Alexander Graydon, Ethan Allen, and, most famously, Benjamin Franklin, since all of necessity select and shape details to conform to the picture of the self the writer seeks to offer.

Among the many paradoxes that flow from the attempt of an admitted confidence man to gain his reader's belief in the truth of what he reports, none, perhaps, is stronger than this: during his career he represented himself as other than what he really was— as a minister, for example, when he was actually the runaway son of a minister—but in each of these representations he successfully became what he represented himself to be—he could, for example, fulfill the duties of a schoolmaster—so that the discovery he was not what he claimed to be was, at the same time, a denial that he was what he had actually become and an insistence that he be what he no longer was. Burroughs's career presented a gaudy caricature of a democratic society's belief that regardless of origin, through skill and application any man can rise in life. He took outrageous shortcuts, but the fact that he could minister or keep a school as successfully as his predecessors in the same posts called into question the nature of true

identity in a socially and geographically mobile society. What
justice attached to the insistence that a man's real nature was
apart from what could be inferred from his actions? Was there
not a point at which the alleged deceiver so inhabited the deception that truth resided in his represented self and error in society's insistence that he cease being what he had become and
revert to what he no longer was? In the *Memoirs,* Burroughs
keeps insisting that he wants only to be permitted to perform the
duties he has proven he can perform well, and comic as are
many of the episodes he recounts, they add up to a pathetic picture of a man constantly anxious, constantly hounded, constantly
hungry, constantly desperate because, finally, he himself does not
know who he is if he is not permitted to be who he says he is.

Brief as was Burroughs's career, its outline is rather lengthy.
The son of the Reverend Eden Burroughs, minister of the church
at Hanover, New Hampshire, and a trustee of Dartmouth College,
he played out the proverbial role of the minister's son as the wildest
boy in town. He was constantly in trouble for one or another prank,
most of them boyish tricks such as stealing from watermelon patches
but all of them touched by a quality that was to continue to tincture
his more mature schemes: a deliberate aim to discomfit authority.
It was not enough, for example, that he stole the watermelons; it
was also necessary that he make publicly ridiculous the elders who
sought to thwart him.

When Burroughs was fourteen he made several unsuccessful
attempts to join the revolutionary army without parental approval
before being sent to the aptly named Coventry in Connecticut, there
to prepare for college under the tutelage of the Reverend Joseph
Huntington. He entered Dartmouth in 1781 but left in the second
quarter of his second year because of what he called an alliance of
his tutors against him. Burroughs does not deny that there may
have been good cause for such an "alliance," and in his account one
can again detect that he aimed pranks that might otherwise have

been dismissed as undergraduate high jinks beyond the fun to the deliberate mocking of authority.

In disgrace, he was provided by his father with twenty dollars and a horse and made his way to the sea coast, where he enlisted on a privateer. When that vessel returned to port after its voyage, Burroughs was arrested and detained on suspicion of theft, a crime for which, he claimed, he was framed by a mate who resented his insubordination.

Burroughs drifted back to Hanover, then went into Massachusetts where he taught school at Haverhill only to be discharged when his Dartmouth tutor learned of his situation and informed the Haverhill authorities of his reputation. Back home at Hanover he continued his misdemeanors. One of them, the robbing of a beehive, seems innocuous enough although it was to become one of the standard features of the legend that soon attached to him, perhaps because the escapade resonated as a metaphor of Burroughs's capacity to prey upon the industrious. Another adventure, the wooing of a woman, was less innocuous since, it turned out, she had a husband, although Burroughs claims he did not know this. At any rate, he was again compelled to leave home.

This second exile began the "notorious" career. What, he asks, was he to do? It was too late in the season to procure a school and he had not the money to enter upon business or study law or medicine:

> There is one thing, said contrivance, which you may do; and it will answer your purposes;—preach. Preach? What a pretty fellow am I for a preacher? A pretty character mine to tickle the ears of a grave audience! Run away from my own home for being connected in robbing a bee house, and for my attention to a married woman; having been through scenes of tumult, during my whole career, since I have exhibited on the active stage of life [a favorite phrase of his for viewing his career]. Besides all this, what appearance should I make in my present dress? which consisted of a light grey coat, with silver-plated buttons, green vest, and red velvet breeches.[4]

Contrivance, however, seems to have counseled him earlier than he acknowledges because, one soon discovers, on leaving home he had prudently armed himself with ten of his father's manuscript sermons. Although he could not immediately remedy his dress, he could put some distance between himself and the place where he was known, change his name, and talk plausibly to those seeking a minister. The picture that emerges from this and subsequent episodes is one of rural villagers so orthodox as to require a minister and so tight-fisted as to want him on niggardly terms that did not permit them to insist upon impeccable credentials. Burroughs was adept at drawing out people in conversation and this talent he converted into a technique. He first talked with a minister in the vicinity to learn what vacancies existed and gain a sense of the profession as it was practiced in the area, next went to the village that sought a minister, boarded with a family that took lodgers, and engaged in extended chats with its members to acquire profiles of the most influential citizens and an anatomy of local prejudices. Once aware of what he called the "genius" of the people, he applied for and received the post of minister of the church of Pelham, Massachusetts, on a week-to-week trial basis.

Matters went on well for several weeks, but Burroughs was put to an increasing number of evasions because of accidental encounters with those who had known him in New Hampshire, until he met one who he was certain would betray him. Consequently, he fled Pelham at night but the next day was discovered in the town of Rutland by a group of irate Pelhamites who had set out in pursuit. A comic footrace ensued, the Rutland locals following in high amusement, until Burroughs was cornered on a hay mow in a barn, at which point he seized a scythe snath and threatened to kill the first man who approached him. The Rutlanders then stepped in, pacified all parties, and negotiated Burroughs's right to flee the district. Several years later while in jail, Burroughs was so impressed by the tales that were circulating—which had him not only standing off the Pelhamites but also, as their minister, preaching them a sermon in the Rutland barn—that he entered into the role assigned him and composed what came to be known as his Hay Mow Sermon. The text was, "Thou shalt seek me, but I shall not be." He subsequently published the sermon in 1798, the same year in which he published his *Memoirs*.

Reflecting on the Pelham incident, Burroughs, whose *Memoirs* is punctuated with philosophical comments on life very much in the vein of Edward Young's *Night Thoughts,* a work he often quoted, reasoned thus with his reader:

> An imposter, we generally conceive, puts on feigned appearances in order to enrich or aggrandize himself, to the damage of others. That this is not the case with me, in this transaction, I think is clear. That I have aimed at nothing but a bare supply of the necessities of life, is a fact. That I have never, in one instance, taken advantage of the confidence which the people of Pelham entertained towards me, to injure them and benefit myself, is a truth acknowledged by all. Under these circumstances, whether I ought to bear the name of imposture, according to the common acceptation, is the question? (*Memoirs*, p. 67)

He had a right to preach, he insists, and others had a right to listen. His only wrong, if wrong it was, was false appearance.

After his flight Burroughs returned secretly to Pelham, there to meet with his one remaining friend in town, a man who had access to counterfeit coins and now urged Burroughs to pass them. In so doing he gave Burroughs a lecture on finance that reads very much like the arguments offered by such as Benjamin Franklin for the issuance of paper currency. It went, in part, as follows:

> Gold and silver are made use of for convenience, to transact our business of barter and exchange with each other, as the representation of property, it being less cumbersome, and more easy to communicate from one to another, than real property of any kind:

hence when there is a due proportion of representative property, business can be transacted to the greatest advantage, and with the greatest ease. And when the public experience a scarcity or redundancy, they of course suffer an inconveniency: therefore, that person who contributes his mite to keep the balance between these two species of property justly poised, is a blessing to himself, and the community of which he is a member. (p. 84)

Since cash is now scarce, Burroughs is told, both self and community are served by increasing its amount. This argument overwhelms his initial contention that the laws of the mind are violated by counterfeiting because acceptance of the protection of civil laws implies agreement to their strictures.

In consenting to pass the false coins, Burroughs reveals to the reader a circumstance that he himself seems never fully to have appreciated, his own susceptibility to deception. It is clear from the text that his friend is sufficiently doubtful that the coins will pass and sufficiently certain that Burroughs, if apprehended, will nevertheless not betray him, that he sends Burroughs on the errand. And, indeed, Burroughs is arrested in Springfield at his first attempt to use the money, put in jail, tried, and convicted.

The local newspapers quickly connected the counterfeit passer with the counterfeit minister of Pelham, and in reports picked up and printed by many another newspaper added to the Burroughs lore by, for example, stating that he had stolen a watch and suit of clothes from a clergyman who had befriended him. Before the court, Burroughs attempted to set the record straight—to acknowledge that he did what he did but deny that he did other deeds reported of him—but he failed. "I do believe," he wrote, "if I had set out with warmth to prove to the world that I was a man, and not a woman, that a great number, from that circumstance would have been able at once to look through the deception which I was endeavoring to lay them under, and known for certainty that I was, in reality, a woman: so strong was the desire of mankind, at that day, to elude my deceptions, which they thought I was master of, to the utmost degree" (p. 94).

The represented Burroughs had swallowed the immanent Burroughs. He could only be who he was represented to be and so powerfully did this circumstance operate that he, indeed, finally capitulated. He wrote the Hay Mow Sermon because he was said to have delivered it, and although the *Memoirs* was designed to clear the record, by the time he wrote it the work was but another version of Burroughs as reported; "true identity" was a term without a referent.

Transferred from Springfield to a more secure jail in Northampton to serve out his sentence, Burroughs made several unsuccessful attempts to escape, including one attempt to burn down the jail. So ingenious were his efforts that despite his failures his reputation as a master of devices grew and he was transferred to the state's most secure prison, that on Castle Island in Boston Harbor, guarded by the United States army. As he made his manacled procession to Boston in an open cart, people gathered along the route to see him. Once at Castle Island he engineered a successful escape to the mainland only to be detected and returned to prison, where he organized an armed uprising. Finally, the prison governor pacified him by agreeing that in exchange for his promise not to escape he would not be confined to a cell but allowed what may paradoxically be called the freedom of the prison.

A pattern had been set and Burroughs's career after his discharge from prison, although packed with event, may be quickly summarized because that pattern asserted itself time and again. He would succeed in getting a foothold in some New England or Long Island town, once as a doctor, thereafter as a schoolmaster, would do well at his profession, then lose his position when his identity was discovered, when, that is, the community insisted upon his being the represented Stephen Burroughs rather than the man who had lived as a member of it. Meanwhile, he encountered a growing number of Stephen Burroughs tales, heard of Stephen Burroughs just having been recognized in some other town, and even met a man who claimed to be Stephen Burroughs. Whenever he was detected, the villagers among whom he had been living harmoniously suddenly managed to remember that aspects of his conduct which they had previously let pass unremarked were actually criminal—especially his liaisons with women. At one point he was charged with rape, but the evidence was so flimsy that the bench of three judges, outraged as they were by the presence before them of *the* Stephen Burroughs, nevertheless could not convict. But they did jail him for lewd behavior. By this time, the notorious villain and the heroic scamp of legend had become so intertwined and the crowds who came to see him at Worcester jail were so admiring that he was allowed to walk free without serving his sentence.

Finally, Burroughs left the northeast, taught school in Georgia, and then became an agent for Robert Morris, the Philadelphia financier, in the large land schemes he was projecting in the southeast. Burroughs had found the right, nominally legal, outlet for his talent and prospered in the office only to lose all when Morris's paper empire collapsed into bankruptcy. The *Memoirs* ends at this point, and biographical information about Burroughs's subsequent career is scanty if intriguing. It is known he moved to Canada and taught school there; it is suggested he also did some trafficking in counterfeit money, but whether such contentions arise from the familiar pattern of requiring the man Burroughs to live up to the represented Burroughs is not clear.

Memoirs provides a curious parallel to William Godwin's *Caleb Williams* (1794), a novel that was much admired in the United States and that influenced the work of Charles Brockden Brown among others. Whether Burroughs had read *Caleb Williams* is unknown;

certainly he was, as both his statements and his citations indicate, an avid reader of contemporary English literature (indeed, at one point fearing that the successive woes he details will weary his reader he says he recognizes that his story, like Richardson's *Clarissa,* is vulnerable to the charge of want of variety).

In *Caleb Williams,* Godwin presents an extended dramatization of the Platonic exercise of tracing the career of virtue in a society that regards it as vice. Common Caleb's true character cannot speak for itself because his actions are repeatedly countered by the representations of him made by his arch foe, Falkland, an aristocrat so revered for his manifest benevolence that the notion he would persecute an innocent man is unthinkable. Appearance wrapped in authority is too powerful for the truth that has no appeal beyond itself. Falkland is, indeed, a benevolent man, but he fell from honor once and that fall is known only to the powerless Caleb. As a consequence, Falkland seeks to discredit every aspect of Caleb's life, employing an agent to find him out so as to disclose to the members of whatever community he inhabits, however blamelessly, that he is the villain who dared to slander the unimpeachable Falkland. Like Burroughs, nothing Caleb actually does can counter the identity assigned him by report.

At a time when the French revolutionary spirit was loose in England, Godwin's aim was to offer a powerful picture of the way in which false social ideals—ideals such as those valorized in Edmund Burke's notorious praise of aristocracy, an established church, and national prejudices—held the English people in fetters they themselves could burst if they but pursued reason rather than inherited beliefs. In his address to Falkland, Williams speaks for Godwin's view of the false ideals that govern Britain:

> Falkland! thou enteredst upon thy career with the purest and most laudable intentions. But thou imbibedst the poison of chivalry with thy earliest youth; and the base and low-minded envy

that met thee on thy return to thy native seats, operated with this poison to hurry thee into madness. Soon, too soon, by this fatal coincidence were the blooming hopes of thy youth blasted for ever! From that moment thou only continuedst to live in the phantom of departed honour.[5]

Unlike Caleb Williams, Burroughs is a self-confessed deceiver and he cannot offer his career as an explicit example of the injustice of the social ideals that govern democratic America. But the implicit message is there, dramatized by Burroughs's attempts to be what he says he is rather than what he was. The authority of inherited position has been replaced by the authority of public opinion, but the new authority also dilutes reason with prejudice. In the America of Burroughs's *Memoirs,* society is so unfixed by the doctrines of equality and opportunity that it is forced to rely upon appearance as the basis of judgment yet is made uneasy by the sense that there is a reality that does not meet the eye, although it lacks a shared idea of what that reality may be.

This play of appearance that must be accepted for want of another reality yet cannot be trusted, since it is detached from the facts of immanence that had determined judgments previously, is prominent in a range of writings that center on late-eighteenth-century American life. Examples in Benjamin Franklin's *Autobiography* are abundant and close to notorious. "In order to secure my Credit and Character as a Tradesman," he writes, "I took care not only to be in *Reality* Industrious & frugal, but to avoid all *Appearances* to the Contrary."[6] Here, to be sure, we may argue that Franklin got it right where Burroughs got it wrong since he labors (and counsels others) to make the appearance conform to the reality rather than the reverse. Still, we can ask, in a society that is increasingly shaped by social utility, what is the difference? While the represented self, Franklin implies, is only an accurate presentation of what is really there, the dominant sense of his advice is that society receives its opinion from appearances and these must be worked at rather than relied upon to emerge naturally. Even the "true" self must be fashioned into a representation.

So, in his "Advice to a Young Tradesman Written by an Old One," Franklin writes:

> The most trifling Actions that affect a man's Credit, are to be regarded. The Sound of your Hammer at Five in the Morning or Nine at Night, heard by a Creditor, makes him easy Six Months longer.... Finer Cloaths than he or his Wife wears, or greater Expence in any particular than he affords himself, shocks his Pride, and he duns you to humble you. Creditors are a kind of People, that have the sharpest Eyes and Ears, as well as the best Memories of any in the World. (*Writings,* p. 321)

The assumption underlying the advice is that the tradesman can be truly industrious yet unsuccessful because he does not sufficiently seem to be industrious. Franklin does not suggest that the mere appearance of industriousness will suffice, but if that young tradesman were not industrious yet worked at five in the morning or nine at night the appearance, as in Burroughs's case, might well convert into the reality.

It is notable that Franklin's advice aims at the securing of credit, the lifeblood of trade and, increasingly (as confidence), the lifeblood of community in a society governed by trade. A man is as good as the amount of trust he can command rather than the amount of property he possesses, which, indeed, is not fully effective, however large it may be, unless augmented by the credit it can gain. He coins his good reputation in the form of notes and if his reputation fails, then, like counterfeit money his notes become valueless because unbacked. Burroughs's paradigm is telling: the one unquestionably criminal act he performed was the passing of counterfeit coin; the greatest financial success he enjoyed was in the legal sale of land never seen by either buyer or seller but sufficiently represented for them by paper. Both activities depended for their success upon obtaining confidence from the market, and both collapsed when that confidence was withheld. The practices of the commercial world that Crèvecoeur and Jefferson believed could be kept subordinate to the immanent world of the freehold farmer dominated the economy and, as a consequence, profoundly affected the way in which people represented themselves and measured one another.

~eeeeeeeeQ999eeee~

Many, perhaps most, of the novels of the period, whether English or American, followed the Richardsonian pattern and centered on the theme of the disasters that followed from seduction. The seducers are archetypical confidence men, but it would seem a distortion to relate the popular appeal of the theme of a virgin's ruin to the advent of the paper-based economy that brought increasing power to the middle class did these novels not, as they do, contextualize the central seduction with economic details. A strong example is provided by *Charlotte Temple* (1791; first American edition, 1794) which, indeed, in the career of its author and the history of its reception also exemplifies the mutual attraction that existed between its themes and the unarticulated anxieties of American society.[7] Susanna Rowson wrote the novel in her native England before imitating her central characters in moving to the United States in 1793. There she continued to write while working first as a professional actress and then for the last twenty-five years of her life (she died in 1824) as headmistress of the young ladies' academy she had founded. Meanwhile, *Charlotte Temple* entered upon a career that saw it become the most frequently published novel of nineteenth-century America with over two hundred editions. In it, the heroine, Charlotte, is persuaded to leave her boarding school in England and accompany her wooer, Montraville, to America where he will serve in the British army. She assumes he will marry her, but he abandons her in her pregnancy and she dies shortly after giving birth to a daughter.

In her preface, Rowson says she wrote "with a mind anxious

for the happiness of that sex whose morals and conduct have a powerful influence on mankind in general," a conventional but not necessarily insincere disclaimer common to novelists of the genre (p. iv). It also establishes a physical fact, female virginity, as an undeniable reality against which appearance can be measured. In the world of the seduction novel, unlike that of commerce, appearance and reality cannot be reversed—chaste behavior cannot restore lost chastity. The everyday reality of the eighteenth-century American reader in which, as was noted, probably one in three women was pregnant before her marriage gave contrary evidence: although in point of physical fact virginity once lost could never be regained, more broadly speaking a moral, socially useful life was available to the "fallen" woman even as it was available to a man who had misconducted himself earlier in life. But the seduction novel is notorious for its insistent hounding of its heroine to death even while, at the same time, it assumes the privilege of standing beside the deathbed and weeping. Why?

The economic details with which such novels abound suggest that the answer resides in the assignment of the role of lost immanence to women by a society that yearned for an absolute behind the appearances that seemed to have replaced it in all transactions. Women were put into the position of embodying the quality of a fixed reality that had disappeared from the everyday world of getting a living; their chastity figured in the plot as a determinate value in a world in which the worth of most things was indeterminate. The novel of seduction typically concerns itself with a negative example; the woman cannot preserve the true value she represents and as a result dies. The repetition of such negative examples in popular novels suggests indulgence in nostalgia for a world that is no longer rather than an obsession with female chastity.

Charlotte Temple's father was the younger son of an earl, and his brother, who would inherit the title, married for money to prop the sinking wealth of their ancient family. Temple had also seen "his sisters legally prostituted to old decrepid men" toward the same end. In a society in which portable wealth had overwhelmed landedness he nevertheless vowed to keep the old ways and seek what he called "content." Accordingly, he rejected a marriage to a wealthy woman arranged by his father, who then banished him from the family seat; he married for love, and, for a time, found contentment in a rural cottage with his Lucy.

This Lucy was the daughter of Eldridge, a respectable retired army officer whose tale within the larger tale mirrors its theme. Eldridge unsuspectingly accepted a generous loan from a man named Lewis in order to assist his son's career, only to learn that Lewis expected Lucy Eldridge to become his mistress in exchange. Eldridge, that is, had unwittingly borrowed with his daughter's virginity as collateral. When he learned of Lewis's design he spurned it, and Lewis then foreclosed, sending Eldridge off to debtors prison. Temple, hearing of the plight of a worthy man who was a stranger to him, visited him in prison and out of sheer benevolence to mankind in general redeemed Eldridge's note at the cost of a good portion of his already straitened income. Made wary by Lewis's behavior, Eldridge suspected Temple of a similar design on Lucy's virtue, but Temple replied that although in the course of his acquaintance with the Eldridges he had come to love Lucy and wished to marry her, his redemption of Eldridge's debt was unconditional. Happily, Lucy also loved him and they married, but this exemplary true-love marriage, the only one in the novel, is, nevertheless, also accompanied by a financial transaction.

Charlotte is the only child of Lucy and Temple. Montraville, her seducer, is, as Temple had been, forbidden by his father to marry unless he marries wealth. Without even the modest income of Temple, the only way he can possess Charlotte is as his mistress, since his financial well-being depends upon his remaining available for marriage to an heiress. Accordingly, he promises Charlotte marriage in order to possess her and once he has succeeded makes some trifling accommodation for her and moves on to marry wealth. The one positive example standing against the vicious marriages and liaisons that abound in the novel is that of Lucy and Temple, but not only does their marriage involve a financial transaction but that marriage can be happily sustained only in a retreat from society that proves, finally, to be temporary when the wider world in the person of Montraville tests it.

It is significant that while the men in *Charlotte Temple* plan and operate on the basis of their ability to represent themselves credibly, Charlotte, around whom the action swirls, is not permitted such an augmentation of her character.[8] She represents nothing beyond her virginity; her real self and her apparent self are identical; when she loses her virtue there is no Charlotte left over. Late in the novel she attempts to represent her position by sending letters home to her family from America, but they are intercepted by the villainous Belcour and never reach their destination. This interception, a minor piece of plot machinery, symbolizes a larger if buried theme, that of Charlotte's inability to construct a self-narrative that in organizing her experience for her permits her to assimilate and survive it. She is blocked from entering the world of representation and held to being only her chastity; once that is lost she has reached her end.

Rowson appears to recognize the conflict between the ideology of female immanence she preaches and the realities of her reader's world because she offers contrasting messages when she speaks directly to her reader. From within the tale she talks, for example, to those whom she expects to be impatient with the triumphs of vice and defeats of virtue: "Remember, the endeavours of the wicked are often suffered to prosper, that in the end their fall may be attended with more bitterness of heart; while the cup of affliction is poured out for wise and salutary ends," the principal one of which is a mansion in the kingdom of eternity (p. 170). But from a position a step farther outside the plot and a step closer inside the reader's everyday world, she offers skeptical advice very much in the vein of Poor Richard's empirical observations: "the only way to ensure the friendship and assistance of your surrounding acquaintances is to convince them you do not require it" (p. 175).

The imbalance between the values enforced by the emotional pattern of the plot and the shrewd practical advice the author offers from outside it suggests that the context of the novel of seduction was coming close to overwhelming its text of lost chastity. Society's shift from real to personal (that is, represented) property and the unsettling of the values previously attached to a distinction between reality and appearance compromised, if indeed they did not dominate, the simple story of innocence betrayed.

The period's most accomplished novelist, Charles Brockden Brown, acutely registered the social shift that had led to context dominating text in the popular genre of the seduction novel and sought to reverse the two. He experimented with plots in which matters of identity and self-representation were central and episodes of seduction contextual.

Wieland (1798), for example, is a novel about the ambiguity of appearances and the difficulty of arriving at a stable reality even after appearance is penetrated. Here a tale within the tale offers the conventional seduction plot. But the main plot centers on the potentially treacherous nature of appearances as they affect all members of society rather than as they lead to seduction. In *Wieland*, as in a second of his major novels, *Edgar Huntly* (1799), Brown constructs characters who either plead guilty to past misdemeanors but insist they are no longer the vicious persons they once were or admit the existence of evidence that impugns their integrity but insist that it should be interpreted in another fashion. Such characters offer self-narratives that, in effect, claim to contain the truth that evades a mere recital of the facts. They maintain that truth does not reside in what meets the eye but in the interpretations that address the reason.

A useful light on the procedure is provided by the convention in portrait painting which held that the pictured details of the physical presence of the sitter could not reach at the inner truth. Accordingly, the sitter was surrounded with items that emblematized his mind. Ezra Stiles, for example, said of the books amidst which he sat in his portrait (each title of which was visible), the pattern on the wall over his head, and the black spot on his left side, "These Emblems are more descriptive of my Mind than the Effigies of my Face."[9] Stiles was a minister who believed that identity was stable and resided in the mind which, being invisible to the outer eye, required the assistance of symbols for its representation. But Brown was an urbanite, trained in the law, and for him identity was fluid and resided in the dynamic relationship between motive and act. The way he reached this in his novels was through the self-narratives of his characters. The speaker spoke her or his life and the fact that what she or he spoke differed from what met the eyes of others located identity in a subjective condition ever liable to change. In Brown the self-narratives that are most telling are not those that frame the novel, not, that is, the first-person viewpoint through which the entire story is told, but the accounts the characters give of themselves to other characters within the novel. Such accounts illustrate the narrator's constantly shifting adjustment to the data of personal experience so as both to conform them to what he is and to adapt himself to what they have made him become. Self-narratives in Brown, that is, collapse the representer into what he represents and prevent our evaluating his account in terms of such absolutes as truth and falsehood, virtue and vice.

Although in this regard Brown seems to have been influenced by Rousseau finally he differs markedly from him. Rousseau wrote in his *Confessions:*

I may omit facts, transpose events, and fall into some errors of dates, but I cannot be deceived in what I have felt, nor in that which from sentiment I have done; and to relate this is my chief aim. The real object of my confessions is to communicate an exact knowledge of what I essentially am and have been in every situation of my life. I have promised the history of my mind, and to write it faithfully I have no need of other aids: to enter into my own heart, as I have hitherto done, will be sufficient.[10]

Certainly one or another of Brown's characters seems forever to be offering his auditors entry into his heart as the way of perceiving the truth of events, which, if they were viewed from the outside, would implicate him in misconduct. But the truth that erases the omissions and errors of Rousseau's account is, as in religious confession, the awareness of an "I" that persists in its essential features despite the shift of events. Fidelity to the revelation of this essential self is the driving principle of his narrative. Brown's self-narrators, on the other hand, know no "I" that persists, know no self other than that built up by—rather than revealed by—their narratives, and their omissions and errors are to be erased by the knowledge that they no longer are what they were even as they are still on the road to what they will be. There is no assumed real self that is being represented; rather, the representation creates the only self there is. In uncertain, mobile American society, long on opportunities and short on achievements, the story of an individual is the story of the way he negotiates the facts of experience to become the self he represents himself as being.

Arthur Mervyn (1799) is that novel of Brown's in which the issue of the truth of self-representation most fully absorbs both the manner and matter of the work. It opens in 1793 in the nightmare city of Philadelphia, where the yellow fever epidemic rages. Houses stand vacant, either abandoned by those who have fled to the country or left open to looting by the deaths of their occupants. Carts roam the ill-lit streets searching for corpses to take to the burial ground

and for fevered fugitives too feeble to resist being snatched and
trundled off to Bush Hill, the hellhole that is the municipal hospital
whence scarcely any emerge alive.

Dr. Stevens, the initial narrator, has remained in the city to apply
his medical skills to the desperate situation, and returning home one
night he encounters a young man leaning against a wall, obviously
stricken with the fever. That youth's simple and ingenuous aspect
and his manlike beauty so strongly impress Stevens that he risks
taking him home to care for him there rather than leaving him to
the death carts. His wife, similarly struck by the young man's appearance of candor and innocence, agrees to shelter and nurse him.

As he convalesces, the youth, Arthur Mervyn, tells the Stevenses
his story. It is the lengthiest of the many self-narratives in the novel.
It is also the first account Arthur in his young life has ever given
of himself, and moved as are the Stevenses, Arthur himself is even
more deeply affected because in the telling he establishes for himself
who he is. In view of these effects, Arthur goes on as the novel
progresses to tell his story of himself to just about every person he
encounters, as if what he is is his account of himself. To meet him
is to hear his story.

That story is one of a lad from the country who, after his mother's
death and his father's remarriage to a scheming village slut, found
himself dispossessed of the family farm and so went to the city to
seek his fortune. There some minor misadventures suffered at the
hands of deceivers cost him what little money and self-confidence
he had, and he resolved to return to the country and bury himself
in rural labor. But on his way out of the city he encountered a man,
Welbeck, who persuaded him to return to Philadelphia as his private
secretary. Apparently a man of great wealth, Welbeck established
Arthur in his mansion, provided him with clothing and the privileges
of the house, and exacted only minor duties from him. As Arthur
came to learn, however, Welbeck was a forger and a swindler who
maintained a wealthy facade in order to prey on the fortunes of

others. He employed Arthur because his resemblance to another young man qualified him for use as a tool in one of his schemes. These details of Welbeck's career are given to Arthur by Welbeck himself at a moment when Welbeck considers himself ruined and so has nothing to lose by telling the truth. But although what Welbeck says of himself is probably true, there is no way for either Arthur or the reader to ascertain that it is certainly so. One who admits that to that point he has lived by false representations is necessarily suspect even in his confessions (as Stephen Burroughs amply illustrates). But beyond this, even if Welbeck is now telling the truth, the past events of his life underscore the realization that like his lies his truths are also relative to a specific situation. Welbeck, in short, illustrates the relativity of all self-narrative, even that of the candid and ingenuous Arthur, and so the mutability of identity.

Thus, in the first part of the novel Stevens's story is quickly swallowed by Arthur's long self-narrative, which contains within it Welbeck's self-narrative. In the second part of the novel, Stevens meets with evidence that calls into question the veracity of Arthur's narrative. A respectable woman who was acquainted with Arthur when he was a boy on his father's farm reports he was lazy and insolent and was once detected in a compromising situation with the woman whom, in his self-narrative, he had characterized as a slut who hated him and alienated his father's affections. Further, a merchant friend of Stevens who had been bilked by Welbeck identifies Arthur as an accomplice in that fraud. Stevens can scarcely believe yet cannot discount such testimony, and Arthur is called upon to explain. Only too willing to do so, Arthur resumes control of the novel with an amplification of his self-narrative that redeems him in the eyes of those who distrusted him. Thus vindicated, he moves on in the novel's present to study medicine with Stevens, marry a woman of means, and plan a life of travel and the observation of human nature preparatory to commencing medical practice. His lengthy explanation is marked by Brown's fondness for plots within plots in a process that at times threatens to become an infinite regression.

The near anarchy of the plague-stricken city in which the central actions occur mirrors a corresponding unhinging of moral values. Who is ill and who is well? Who is what he appears to be? Arthur's first encounter with the woman he will marry takes place in a house of prostitution, yet, as each eventually believes of the other, they were there on innocent errands. The last of the money Welbeck earned by fraud is invested with a respectable merchant in a legal commercial enterprise, yet that respectable merchant defrauds the fraudulent Welbeck who is finally doing something legitimate. Arthur burns a bank note because Welbeck tells him it is forged only then to be told by Welbeck that it was genuine; how was he to know the truth other than by accepting Welbeck's word, which was quickly reversed, or by testing the note on the market, which could have implicated him and others in fraud?

The answers to such questions reside not in objective evidence but in the accounts of events offered by participants. One must listen to another's story and then judge on the basis of that representation rather than on the bare facts it contains. All of importance comes to us through the filter of a character's account of himself, and the focus of concern is judgment of the teller's truth to himself rather than of the truth of his tale.

When Welbeck first engages Arthur he imposes two conditions upon him, both negative. The first is that Arthur must suppress his own history and tell no one that he is a farm lad from the hinterlands of Pennsylvania. The second is that Arthur must never enter the private room in which Welbeck keeps his papers. The injunctions resemble one another in that each prohibits Arthur from attaching the present to the past: in one case his own, in the other Welbeck's, represented by the papers in his locked room. Arthur accepts the injunctions because in his America, he believes, one is not bound by who he was but is free to become whom he will. He reasons that what he wishes for himself but has not yet achieved is more indicative of his real self than is his past condition, and he recalls the fairy tales of his childhood, now perceiving in them a hidden truth about the indeterminacy of identity: "Identity itself frequently depends upon a casual likeness or an old nurse's imposture."[11] He may very well be a rich man's rather than a farmer's son or the someone he now only resembles rather than the someone he was. Welbeck's injunctions seem empowering.

As he adapts to the urban life that fuels his aspirations, Arthur recognizes that success depends upon reputation. He cannot, for example, expose the merchant Thetford's scheme to bilk Welbeck because Thetford has a reputation for probity while Arthur is unknown. He learns, accordingly, to concentrate his energies upon constructing a plausible self. That manner counts more than matter, may, indeed, be matter, is verified for him by Stevens's reaction to his tale. "He that listens to his words," says Stevens of Arthur, "may question their truth, but he that looks upon his countenance when speaking, cannot withhold his faith" (p. 218). So powerfully does Arthur, and in his wake the novel itself, seize the perception that reality is dependent upon the will, that he announces, "Sensations do not precede and suggest, but follow and are secondary to the acts of my mind" (p. 253). He thus cuts through all doubts about the reliability of appearance by asserting his ability to shape the world to the image in his mind. Since he is benevolent, that image is a virtuous one. But the doctrine that informs his behavior is one that may as readily endorse deception. Hence the apt characterizations of Arthur by the two most penetrating modern interpreters of the novel: Norman Grabo calls him "an altruist who always profits personally," and Warner Berthoff calls him "a solid figure of high-minded egocentrism."[12]

In *Arthur Mervyn* Brown presents America as a field of opportunity, but unlike idealists such as Crèvecoeur and Jefferson he locates that field in the social relations attendant upon commercial, urban life rather than in the physical conditions of rural life. Success lies in the ability to construct a reputation and capitalize on it rather than remaining within a self unaugmented by representation; personal property has greater influence than real. From early encomiums on the rural life and its honest labors, Arthur progresses to the belief that it is restrictive and does not permit the liberal extension of the self available in the urban life he comes to prefer. He acknowledges the calculation implied by this change of mind and the loss it may entail: "If reason acquires strength only by the diminution of sensibility," he says, "perhaps it is just for sensibility to be diminished" (p. 269).

The society constituted by Brown's novels is one in which the difference between appearance and reality is uncertain. Commercial, political, and literary representations amplified its power but they also made its members uneasy. Representing and misrepresenting were dangerously alike and the individual's capacity to become other than what he had been was not clearly distinguishable from his capacity to deceive. Stephen Burroughs was the mocking double of Benjamin Franklin, and the persistent popularity of the story of Charlotte Temple, whose fate was irrevocably tied to her immanent self, manifested a deep if unarticulated distrust of the new world in which Arthur Mervyn's representations could so stainlessly erase the past.

CHAPTER FIVE

WRITING FOR PRINT

Benjamin Franklin and Urban Experience—The *Autobiography*, Secrecy, and
Books—Print Culture and Republican Ideology

XAMINING the notorious chart of virtues in Benjamin Franklin's *Autobiography*, Max Weber comments, "According to Franklin those virtues, like all others, are only in so far virtues as they are actually useful to the individual, and the surrogate of mere appearance is always sufficient when it accomplishes the end in view."[1]

His point is well taken, but, then, Franklin made no attempt to disguise his sense of the matter. A virtue such as temperance was indispensable for worldly success because intemperance led to wasteful expenditure and undermined efficiency on the job. The mere appearance of temperance, therefore, would not suffice because even if others regarded the individual as temperate, intemperance itself would have deleterious consequences. On the other hand, humility was necessary only because others are apt to be persuaded by and trust an individual whom they regard as modest more than one who appears arrogant. In this case, then, Franklin admitted, appearance will serve: "I cannot boast of much Success in acquiring the *Reality* of this Virtue, but I had a good deal with regard to the *Appearance* of it."[2]

At the core of Franklin's use of the terms *appearance* and *reality* was his concern with the distinction between the public and the private life. Convinced that both personal success and the welfare of society depend upon the public conduct of individuals, he insisted upon the private development of virtues such as temperance that had an inevitable effect upon public behavior, while he fully admitted that other virtues—humility, for example—were in the keeping of the observer rather than the observed and need not necessarily arise from private character.

To recognize this is to appreciate that to a degree unmatched by any other leader of the new nation, Franklin was formed by the city, by the conditions of trade and the circumstances of daily intercourse with a range of his fellow citizens. Shaped by the city, he was also its shaper, founding the institutions of modern urban life— such as hospitals, schools, fire companies, sanitation agencies, and streetlighting facilities—and advocating patterns of conduct that ensured the advancement of both the individual and society, which, he believed, went hand in hand.

Franklin was raised in Boston where, famously, his father took him on visits to the various tradesmen and craftsmen of the town in order to prepare his mind for the choice of a vocation, and where his apprenticeship to his brother, printer of an intensely political newspaper, gave him daily glimpses into the crucial importance of acting in association with others rather than individually. At the age of sixteen he took this knowledge to Philadelphia, America's largest and the British empire's second largest city, and his developing genius was further shaped by urban conditions when he worked in the empire's largest city, London, in his nineteenth and twentieth years.

The range of experience thus acquired resulted in a conviction of the inseparability of the individual and society, the dependence of private character upon public perception, and the need to associate if one were to succeed. By the standard of the Puritan patriarchs of his native Boston, such a merging of the private and the public was heretical, an obliteration of the central condition of identity, the soul's relation to and dependence upon God. And even those who had drifted from such orthodoxy nevertheless clung to notions of individual identity as ultimately independent of social circumstances. For them, America was a nation of yeoman farmers where the immanent self was formed by daily contact with nature and nature's god; the individual brought such an identity to society and there retained its core inviolable.

Another circumstance related to his urban experience also differentiated Franklin's development from that of his celebrated peers. He had arrived in both Philadelphia and London as a stranger and, accordingly, fashioned himself in terms of what those cities required of young men. For want of other credentials he had to give an account of himself in words and deeds, and the account he gave was what he became. To the moment of his death at the age of eighty-four, when he was renowned throughout the Western world, Franklin was still giving an account of himself. Dictating the final part of his *Autobiography* from his sickbed, he was fashioning the narrative that he thought should stand for—should be—Benjamin Franklin. Although from his day to ours corrections, supplements, and refutations of the details in that narrative have been undertaken on the basis of evidence external to it, still the Franklin of the *Autobiography* is the Franklin of persisting significance because that Franklin incorporates his central perception of the public nature of private character.

The success story that is the core fable of the *Autobiography* is designedly there. With his view of the interdependence of public and private, Franklin's account of himself had also to be an account of his country, not so much of the great public events in which he participated as of the reflexive relationship that existed between his career and the opportunities presented by his homeland. As such, his story has for generations rightly been taken as a manual for success, the best single model of how to achieve wealth and honor.

That pattern requires no further rehearsing. But two of the themes that accompany Franklin's rise from runaway apprentice to internationally renowned sage are worthy of greater attention because they figure largely in his success and yet—amply and frankly present as they are in the *Autobiography*—Franklin does not point to them as he points to many a less significant motif when, from time to time, he generalizes his experience into maxims for those who would benefit from it.

The first theme is the way in which secrecy, sometimes carrying over into duplicity, formed an essential part of his world and played an important role at crucial stages of his career. When, for example, his brother James, to whom he was apprenticed, was forbidden by legal order to print *The New-England Courant,* that paper was continued under the name of Benjamin Franklin, printer, a legalistic maneuver bordering on deceit since the James Franklin who was prohibited from publishing the paper continued to do so by using his apprentice as the nominal publisher. In order to cover the maneuver, James publicly dissolved the apprenticeship while secretly retaining the document that still bound Benjamin to him. When, therefore, Benjamin decided his apprenticeship was intolerable, he fled from it knowing that his brother could not retain him without publicly revealing his evasion of the legal order against his printing the *Courant.* Benjamin took advantage of one deception to practice another.

In Philadelphia the runaway found that Bradford, the printer, had no need for an additional hand, but Bradford's father, on a visit to his son from New York where he too was a printer, volunteered to take the young man to the town's other printer, Keimer, who threatened to be a dangerous commercial rival to his son. The elder Bradford posed as a well-wisher who was bringing Keimer a needed assistant and in this guise drew Keimer out about his plans to surpass Bradford in the Philadelphia market, the young and knowing Ben Franklin meanwhile standing by in silence.

Encouraged by Governor William Keith to set up in rivalry to both Bradford and Keimer, Franklin against his father's advice embarked on the venture and so literally embarked for London to purchase supplies for the new printing establishment. He had no resources for this other than those promised by Keith as forthcoming, but the one letter that he found in the ship's post bag that might possibly have been the promised letter of credit from Keith proved, when he presented it to the royal stationer to whom it was addressed, to have been written by a crony of Keith's who wished to involve the stationer in a political plot against the plans of Andrew Hamilton, a distinguished Philadelphia politician then in London. Contemptuous of the letter's sender, the stationer handed the paper back to Franklin in an abrupt dismissal. Thus abandoned in London, Franklin carried the letter to Hamilton, thereby aiding Hamilton in his plans and establishing an acquaintanceship that eventually led to his benefitting commercially from Hamilton's wide influence. (This betrayal of correspondence foreshadowed the notorious publication of the confidential Hutchinson-Oliver letters years later in London, an incident that does not figure in the *Autobiography*.)

Back in Philadelphia and again employed by Keimer, Franklin entered into an agreement with a fellow employee, Hugh Meredith, to set up a printing establishment financed by Meredith's father. They sent to London for the necessary equipment and meanwhile remained in Keimer's employ, keeping secret the fact that they would soon be his competitors.

Other examples occur, but the foregoing sufficiently reflect that in the commercial and political world in which young Franklin began to advance his career, secrecy and deception were conditions of life; one employed them in order to advance oneself and, almost inevitably, worst others, and one expected that others were employing them against oneself. Franklin draws no general maxims from this in the *Autobiography;* he does not explicitly advise that the world being a treacherous place one must be prepared to do as he is done by (although Poor Richard's proverbs frequently imply this). But since duplicity is a given in the world of the *Autobiography*, if its practice is not recommended neither is it condemned. It is simply a morally neutral fact of life, and Franklin treats it neither rancorously when it operates against him nor gleefully when it operates for him. Keith deceived him, but then, he shrugs, Keith having nothing else to give gave expectations. Franklin wastes no energy in preaching against Keith's practice; he simply turns around and betrays a private letter into the hands of Keith's enemies. The prominence of secrecy in the affairs of Franklin's world is especially noteworthy in view of the fact that he was a printer and so a publisher by trade, that is, one whose business it is to make things public, and the relation between the secret and the printed will receive attention farther along in the discussion.

The second prominent theme of the success story in the *Autobiography* that is never elevated into an explicit maxim is the *social* advantages that adhere to the possession and reading of books. The narrative abounds in examples of the practical part played by reading in self-improvement: through it Franklin learned how to write, how to dispute, and even how to plan his meals. And reading, of course, educated him into the many fields his genius mastered. But in addition, books were his passport to social and thence to commercial and political advancement. He received an early indication of this when as a runaway of suspicious appearance he stopped at an inn in New Jersey and there began a lifelong friendship with its owner, Dr. Brown, when the older man discovered that the youth owned and read books. On a return journey to Boston, Franklin, still an unknown, was summoned to the home of Governor Burnet of New York because the governor had heard from the captain of the ship on which Franklin arrived that there was a young man aboard who owned a number of books. "The Governor treated me with great Civility," Franklin wrote, "show'd me his Library, which was a very large one, & we had a good deal of Conversation about Books & Authors" (p. 1,336). When Keimer received the commission to print

New Jersey's paper currency, he and Franklin went to Burlington and in a three-month stay there executed the job under the close supervision of members of the colony's legislature. "My mind having been more improv'd by Reading than Keimer's," Franklin wrote, "I suppose it was for that Reason my Conversation seem'd to be more valu'd. They had me to their Houses, introduc'd me to their Friends and show'd me much Civility.... These Friends were afterwards of great Use to me" (p. 1,358). When his rise in Philadelphia was substantially forwarded by his appointment as printer to the Pennsylvania Assembly, Franklin learned that a new member of that body who promised to be influential was opposed to his continuing as printer. He therefore set out to win him over: "Having heard that he had in his Library a certain very scarce & curious Book, I wrote a Note to him expressing my Desire of perusing that Book, and requesting he would do me the Favour of lending it to me for a few Days. He sent it immediately, and I return'd it in about a Week, with another Note expressing strongly my sense of the Favour" (p. 1,403). Thus began another lifelong and politically profitable friendship.

Franklin's interest in books and his conversion of private reading into a body of knowledge superior to any university education available in America were not matters of calculated social climbing, although the mere fact of being familiar with books certainly gained him access to a higher social circle. He reached beyond this to establish the emerging class of ambitious, self-taught trades- and craftsmen as the deciding cultural and political force in American society. In a world in which money to acquire and leisure to read books were marks of the elite class he was displacing, Franklin had to avoid the appearance of leisure appropriate to that class—"a Book, indeed, sometimes debauch'd me from my Work; but this was seldom, snug, & gave no Scandal" (p. 1,369)—even as he benefited from the entry into the company of the influential that his reading afforded him.

Yet further still, books engaged his imagination in excess of any goal. The manuscript of the *Autobiography* consists of four parts. The first was written in England in 1771, the second in France in 1784, and the last two in Philadelphia in 1788, part four consisting of only three final paragraphs. Neither when he resumed his narrative in France after a lapse of thirteen years nor when he resumed it again in Philadelphia after a lapse of four years did Franklin have the previous parts before him. His memory of what he had written earlier had to suffice, and it is therefore striking that as he rummaged in his mind for the points at which to resume, in both instances, uncertain of whether or not he was repeating himself, he decided upon books as the topic that was the most important to be included if, by chance, he had omitted it, or the least annoying to repeat if, by chance, he had already mentioned it. The first part closes with an account of how his friends and he founded the first subscription library in North America, and the second part commences with a similar account. Stirring his imagination to generate the third part, Franklin again turned to books and commenced with "Observations on my Reading History in Library."

—eeeeeeeQQeeeeeee—

Viewed objectively, the two ungeneralized yet encompassing themes of the *Autobiography,* secrecy and books, are not any more closely related to each other than they are to other features of Franklin's world. But viewed subjectively, as phenomena integrated by his life, they cohere into the essence of his character. Franklin was a printer, and beyond others of his day, even fellow printers, he comprehended the cultural revolution that print was effecting. To publish is to make public in a multitude of identical copies that have the effect of depersonalizing discourse and transferring authority from the speaker to the spoken. To replicate in print is to translate self into the general. Printing, to be sure, had been established centuries before Franklin took up the trade, but his America was contemporary with, and to a marked extent the consequence of, the spread of print from centers of learning or population into the countryside of towns and villages. Print was put to an increasing number of uses as a growing proportion of the population relied upon reading for instruction and amusement, and the printing press followed the flow of settlement, becoming an institution of daily life. Clearly, the democratization of print both promoted and was promoted by the democratization of society.

Although many writers were slow to grasp the fact, there was a difference between a written piece that was later printed and a piece written deliberately to be printed. They proceeded from the assumption that the writer—because of his rank, learning, or office— was in a position of authority relative to his readership and that that readership was a determinate body of interested persons. To the extent that such assumptions operated, the literate culture which had replaced oral culture was still not yet print culture.

But Franklin did grasp the features that distinguished modern print culture. He saw that print's capacity to diffuse information, thought, and sentiment beyond the limits of place and moment meant that it need not address an audience conceived of as a determinate group, such as the members of a religious denomination, occupation, or social class, but could cross such boundaries in constructing its readership. The new group constituted by a readership was indeterminate because made up of individuals who, by and large, neither knew nor lived in proximity to one another, yet it possessed the power of its numbers and could be made to weigh as heavily as more determinate groups.

From his perception of the implications of print for written discourse, Franklin twitted the two groups, clergymen and lawyers, who dominated written discourse but failed to grasp the nature of print. Targeting the sermon, the preeminent oral performance of his day, Franklin lampooned its format once it was viewed in cold print, saying of the publishing preachers:

Let them have the Liberty of repeating the same Sentence in other Words; let them put an Adjective to every Substantive, and double every Substantive with a Synonima, for this is more agreeable than hauking, spitting, taking Snuff, or other Means of concealing Hesitation. Let them multiply Definitions, Comparisons, Similitudes, and Examples. Permit them to make a Detail of Causes and Effects, enumerate all the Consequences, and express one Half by Metaphor and Circumlocution. Nay, allow the Preacher to tell us whatever a Thing is negatively, before he begins to tell what it is affirmatively; and suffer him to divide and subdivide as far as *Two and fiftiethly.*[3]

But when a discourse is to be printed, "bound down upon Paper," as Franklin puts it, then the brief, the perspicuous, and the direct are called for because the discourse must stand without the aid of the speaker's presence.

Similarly, Franklin lampooned the verbosity of legal writings in a day when print made them available to common readers: "you must abridge the Performances to understand them; and when you find how little there is in a Writing of vast Bulk, you will be as much supriz'd as a Stranger at the opening of a Pumpkin."[4] In short, Franklin knew that print meant a readership for sermons that was not to be treated as if they were sitting unquestioningly under the minister's gaze and a readership for legal matters larger than and distinct from those familiar with the professional jargon. The principle could be extended into almost all areas of knowledge.

Franklin's first published writings were designed for his brother's *New-England Courant,* and throughout his career he shaped his writing for an assumed audience of intelligent, busy people who had the ability to understand even technical subjects if they were presented in a clear and simple—even homely—style within the relatively brief compass of the usual journal article. Each of his pieces proceeds from the pen of a persona; none presumes to be written by an individual whose reputation having gone before him establishes the authority of what he says. Each piece must take its independent chance, deriving its effect from what it can work in the reader. Franklin's acknowledged masters, the great English essayists of the early century such as Addison and Swift, had taught him technique. But in one respect at least he went beyond them. Influenced by American conditions he accepted the indeterminate nature of his readership—neither learned nor ignorant; interested in the weather and interested in statistics; alert to personal profit and sympathetic to schemes of social benevolence—and he called forth the audience that from his day to this exists substantially yet elusively under the title of the common reader.

The American world of print that Franklin's mastery shaped is put into relief by the notes of a young scholar who had been formed by it. Studying in Göttingen in 1819, the Massachusetts-born George Bancroft marveled at what he called the "democracy" of German literary culture. America had not prepared him for a land in which a class of men could earn their living by learning and publishing regardless of their birth. In his homeland democratic opportunity extended to economic and social mobility but did not encourage learning as a trade; in Germany, Bancroft noted, "much knowledge is collected that one may have a chance of selling himself at a higher price." There was also, however, a price to be paid. Whereas in America similar knowledge was purveyed to the public by Franklinesque writers whose articles and books were outgrowths of occupations and concerns broader if shallower than those of professional scholars, in Germany, "the learned write for the learned." As a result, while the products of the American press were received as matters of public consequence, in Germany, "the literary class had little or no influence on the people."[5]

The way writing entered into the daily life of the people in the United States may be glimpsed in a range of personal narratives. Recalling his youth in Connecticut at the turn of the century, for example, Samuel Goodrich said that at that time books and newspapers "were read respectfully, as if they were grave matters, demanding thought and attention. They were not ... hastily dismissed, like waste paper.... Even the young approached a book with re-

verence, and a newspaper with awe."[6] And an exasperated Stephen
Burroughs reported on how his efforts to give a true account of
himself were thwarted by those who claimed to know better because
they had read about him in a newspaper and for them the printed
word was far more authoritative than any oral testimony.

Strikingly, as dependent as learning was upon print, a strong
link between education and oral culture nevertheless remained, from
spelling bees and recitations in the lower school grades through to
theses argued in universities. In the patriotic 1770s, those who as-
pired to poetic fame wrote epics of their homeland, more honored,
even in their day, for the fact of the accomplishment than the pleasure
of the reading. John Trumbull, Timothy Dwight, Joel Barlow, "each
wrote," as Kenneth Silverman says in his astute survey of the decade,
"an orotund Augustan progress poem on American empire, gran-
diose in sentiment and climaxed by a boastful vision of the future."
All these poets came from that very small proportion of the population that had attended college, and, as Silverman says, "these
speech-like pieces reflect the tie between oratory and poetry in the
college curriculum, and could be called verse orations."[7]

When Franklin, educated by print outside of collegiate walls,
proposed a university that unlike all then existing in America would
be founded free of sectarian interest and devoted to preparing a
range of young men for the social and economic conditions of their
country rather than to finishing the wealthy and furnishing the
clergy, he was compelled to acknowledge the hold oratory had on
the curriculum. "*History* will show the wonderful Effects of ORA-
TORY," he admitted, "in governing, turning, and leading great Bodies
of Mankind." But that effect had in turn become history, and he
recommended that after the students are "struck with Admiration"
at what oratory had once wrought, and the beauties of the ancient
speeches are pointed out to them, the instructor should move on:
"Modern Political Oratory being Chiefly performed by the Pen and
Press, its Advantages over the Antient in some Respects are to be
shown, as that its Effects are more extensive, more lasting, &c."[8]

The phrase "in some respects" is typical Franklin demurral, the best persona for a proposer being one of modesty and openness to persuasion. In point of fact, his discourse indicates no advantages that speech has over pen and press.

The spread of print culture in America was greeted with dismay by many and misunderstanding by even more. The dismay was felt by those on opposite sides of the day's political controversies, for contrasting reasons. On one hand, there was the remarkable Joseph Dennie, the United States' first full-fledged Miniver Cheevy. From his days in the cradle in Lexington where he was born in 1768 through his Harvard education to his career as a literary journalist, Dennie appears to have had one overwhelming ambition in the pursuit of which he never wavered—to be a great man of letters on the model of such English giants as Samuel Johnson. In Boston in 1791 he founded *The Tablet,* an ambitious literary journal that proved too ambitious. Relocating in Walpole, New Hampshire, the very location an indication of the dispersal of printing, he became editor of the *Farmer's Weekly Museum,* and drawing around him a circle of politically minded wits with literary ambitions, he improved that journal into one that had a readership in all the states and placed it fully in the Federalist camp. In 1799 Dennie moved to Philadelphia where after other journalistic efforts he founded *The Port Folio* in 1801, a magazine that for fifteen years went unrivaled as the best literary journal in the country.

Dennie's view of literary excellence was fixed firmly on English tradition, and his Federalism was an expedient substitute for his true allegiance, which was to a class society of monarch, aristocrats, club wits, and elegant satirists disdainful of the taste of the mob. Writing to his parents in the year before he founded *The Port Folio,* Dennie expressed himself with characteristic acerbity:

> Had not the *Revolution* happened; had I continued a subject to the King, had I been fortunately born in *England* or resided in the City of London for the last 7 years, my fame would have been enhanced;

and as to fortune I feel a moral certainty that I should have acquired by my writings 3 or 4 thousand pounds. But in this *Republic,* this region covered with the Jewish and canting and cheating descendants of those men, who during the reign of a Stuart, *fled away* from the claims of the Creditor, from the tithes of the Church, from the allegiance to their Sovereign and from their duty to their God, what can men of liberality and letters expect but such polar icy treatment as I have experienced?

He went on to make explicit what was already manifest: "foul is the day in our Calendar, and bitterly are those *patriotic* and Indian traitors to be cursed who instigated the *wretched* populace to declare the 4th day of July, 1776, a day of Independence."[9]

No contemporary of Franklin's was nearly so equally qualified to grasp the implications of the spreading print culture as was Dennie. His mother was a Green—Samuel Green (1615–1701) managed the only printing press in the colonies up to 1665 and founded a dynasty of printers made up of his descendants and those trained by them—and so he was a member of one of the most distinguished families in the early history of American printing. He sensed the modifications print required of existing genres. The most popular of his own writings, the lively moralistic essays that first appeared in the *Farmer's Weekly Museum* and were then published and republished in book form (William Cobbett being the first of the book publishers) were titled *The Lay Preacher.* Modeled on the form of the sermon, these pieces were written to be printed, not preached, by a genteel and somewhat dandyish gentleman rather than a pious preceptor. In them Dennie shrewdly conserved the outline of the traditional sermon but abbreviated its length and from his biblical text drew lessons on manners, morals, and politics in place of the doctrinal instruction customarily offered by the clergy.

Viewed from the safe distance of some two centuries, Dennie's outrageous prejudices, expressed with an insistent smirk of superiority, are rather engaging. Especially attractive is an unabashed modernizing of the Bible that translates texts weighted with moral and theological glosses into lessons in modern manners and politics. Franklin did the same occasionally but did so with rather too heavy an allegorical intent. Dennie was defter if more supercilious. Here, for example, is what we should learn from Exodus 6:15–17, the narrative of Moses helping the daughters of Midian to water their flocks:

> Certain shepherds of the country, "fellows of the baser sort," in all probability Midianitish *democrats,* influenced by the wonted churlishness, impudence, boorishness, and ferocity of the republican characters, came and drove those unoffending females away. Perceiving this harshness and, in a spirit of gallantry, resenting it, Moses, with the courtesy of a cavalier, quitted his seat and his meditations, civilly helped the insulted maidens, and relieved them from the labour of watering their flocks.[10]

But Dennie indeed was in the wrong place at the wrong time. He was unable to separate the keen journalistic sense he had acquired through his familiarity with the press from an ideal of literature as the property of the sophisticated few that would inevitably be degraded in direct proportion to the number of persons for whom it was shaped. He spoke often of the "natural malignity of our rascal populace" (*The Lay Preacher,* p. 124). As a consequence, he regarded Franklin as a central villain of the American drama in which circumstances had so cruelly placed him. Politically, he said, Franklin was "the first to lay his head in the lap of French harlotry," and economically Franklin encouraged "a low and scoundrel appetite for small sums" that "degraded our national character." As for his writing, Franklin "was the founder of that Grubstreet sect, who have professedly attempted to degrade literature to the level of vulgar capacities, and debase the polished and current language of books by the vile alloy of provincial idioms, and colloquial barbarism, the shame of grammar and akin to any language rather than English."[11]

Ironically, the shrewdest counter to Dennie's anglophiliac view is not provided by the American "Jacobins" he despised but by a Briton. Writing in the *Edinburgh Review* in 1806, Francis Lord Jeffrey said that Franklin's "style was formed entirely by his own judgment and occasional reading, and most of his moral pieces were written while he was a tradesman, addressing himself to the tradesmen of his native city. We cannot expect, therefore, either that he should write with extraordinary elegance or grace; or that he should treat of the accomplishments, follies, and occupations of polite life. He had not great occasion, as a moralist, to expose the guilt and the folly of gaming or seduction; or to point a poignant and playful ridicule against the lighter immoralities of fashionable life."[12] Jeffrey's concluding observation acutely directs us to the most vulnerable aspect of the work of Dennie and other American belletrists of his day devoted to an ideal of English elegance. The style they admired was formed in expression of the interests of a particular segment of a specifically English society. American society differed, and to pursue the same style in application to it was to address concerns that existed in America only as literary conventions. The "lighter immoralities of fashionable life" were, in America, a shadow cast by a transatlantic substance.

The lesson of Dennie's shortcomings was taken by the young Washington Irving, who shared his basic distaste for democracy and imitated Oliver Oldschool, the editorial persona of *The Port Folio*, in the papers of Jonathan Oldstyle (1802) and in the persona of Launcelot Langstaff of *Salmagundi* (1807), the latter, indeed, based even more particularly on Irving's direct personal impression of Dennie. But Irving soon recognized that actual American society did not provide sufficient material for the full play of such a viewpoint and took himself to England to observe more congenial subject matter.

If some such as Dennie at one end of the political spectrum were dismayed by the literature promoted by American print culture because it degraded literature in a pretense of elevating an incurably vulgar populace, some at the other end were dismayed because print in America was degrading an intelligent populace by feeding it literature beneath its capacity. Charles Jared Ingersoll of Philadelphia wrote poetry (he published a poem in *The Port Folio*), drama, and social treatises. But Jeffersonian republican that he was, he regarded his literary activities as a natural adjunct to his career in law and politics—he served a term in Congress—rather than a profession that deserved support in its own right. For Dennie, a work of literature was an event in the history of literature, a history that enjoyed an essential independence from political history. For Ingersoll, a work of literature grew from the condition of the society in whose history it participated, and in a republic would be, ideally, the expression of the concerns of those who wrote from their experiences in a variety of occupations rather than because they were professional writers. His dismay at the effects of the spread of print culture was therefore addressed to its failure to meet the needs and capacities of a republican readership:

> I consider rational liberty, useful learning, and solid science, more endangered from what is called the freedom of the press, than from all the hosts of ignorance and tyranny. The discovery of printing has been incalculably beneficial to the mass of mankind, but like all other benefits this is susceptible of corruption and abuse. The magazines, reviews, and newspapers that are spreading over the face of Europe and North America, threaten to deface and obliterate every vestige of the good sense and information to be derived from well chosen reading and unprejudiced inquiry. In the United States particularly, where the people in general are so well informed, there is less occasion than in any other country, for these little lights; and more occasion and a better atmosphere, than in any other, for the great luminaries of science and instruction.[13]

For Ingersoll, the press had failed to keep step with the rise of general intelligence consequent upon a democratic revolution; the extramural university of print so vital in a free country had degenerated into a school for scandal. Dennie might well smile and point out that such leveling was inevitable in a nation ruled by public opinion; true literature by definition was restricted to the few. Ingersoll's and Dennie's agreement about the deplorable state of what was printed and their difference as to the remedy defined a cultural conflict that was to continue to vex American society. Was culture a body of artistic values that remained constant through time and superior to social circumstances, or was it the intellectual condition of a particular society at a given moment? Holding the former view, Dennie deplored the debasement of art that followed from attempts to extend it to a larger audience; holding the latter view, Ingersoll wrote: "Poetry, music, sculpture, and painting, may yet linger in their Italian haunts. But philosophy, the sciences, and the useful arts, must establish their empire in the modern republic of letters, where the mind is free from power or fear, on this side of the great water barrier which the creator seems to have designed for the protection of their asylum."[14] The image of asylum echoes the centuries-old concept of America as the refuge of true religion in flight from the corruption of Europe and suggests that in escaping to the American strand literature can well leave belles lettres behind to molder among the ruins that, thankfully, the new world does not contain.

———

John Adams contemplated Franklin's phenomenal fame with a mixture of bafflement, outrage, and envy, yet also with a degree of shrewd penetration. He could not quite put the pieces together. He sensed that that fame was something new in the world of letters because, although it resulted from Franklin's writings, still, unlike the reputation of other men of letters, say of John Locke, it was not confined to readers. "His name was familiar to government and people," Adams said, "to kings, courtiers, nobility, clergy and phi-

losophers, as well as plebians, to such a degree that there was
scarcely a peasant or a citizen, a *valet de chambre,* coachman or
footman, a lady's chambermaid or a scullion in a kitchen, who was
not familiar with it, and who did not consider him as a friend to
human kind." But as he puzzled over why this was so, Adams was
too readily attracted to an answer that hinted at conspiracy:

> He had been educated a printer, and had practiced his art in Boston,
> Philadelphia, and London for many years, where he not only learned
> the full power of the press to exalt and spread a man's fame, but
> acquired the intimacy and the correspondence of many men of that
> profession with all their editors and many of their correspondents.
> This whole tribe became enamoured and proud of Mr. Franklin as
> a member of their body, and were consequently always ready and
> eager to publish any panegyric upon him that they could procure.
> Throughout his whole life he courted and was courted by the print-
> ers, editors, and correspondents of reviews, magazines, journals,
> and pamphleteers, and those little busy meddling scribblers that are
> always buzzing about the press in America, England, France, and
> Holland.[15]

To be sure, Franklin enjoyed excellent relations with the whole
"tribe" connected with printing, but the reasons for his great reputation extended beyond the puffing he thus received. Adams held
the key to a better answer when he noted: "His rigorous taciturnity
was very favorable to this singular felicity. He conversed only with
individuals, and freely only with confidential friends. In company
he was totally silent" (Lemay and Zall, p. 246). Blinded by the way
in which his own reputation had suffered from the press, Adams
left the point unanalyzed and fixed on the more obvious circumstance
of Franklin's standing in the fraternity of printers.

Franklin's celebrated silence seems, indeed, to be at the root of
the matter. Even in deliberative assemblies he spoke infrequently
and then only briefly—never more than "ten minutes at a time, nor
to any but the main point," Jefferson recalled.[16] He acted from a

conviction so deeply held that it was an essential trait of character rather than an idea, a conviction that speech was fittest for private moments and print for public. Since the deliberations in which he participated as a representative were to eventuate in public documents, he aimed at the shaping of those documents rather than the display of his personal views and reserved his force for the closed-door conferences and committees concerned with drafting.

The ideological context of Franklin's outlook is acutely identified in the work of Michael Warner: "Social authority, like truth, holds validity not in persons but despite them; it is located not in the virtuous citizen nor in God nor in the king but in the light of day, in the scopic vision of publicity itself. Thus print—not speech—is the ideal and idealized guardian of civic liberty, as print discourse exposes corruption in its lurking holes but does so without occupying a lurking hole of its own."[17] And Warner amplifies his perception thus: "Developed in practices of literacy that included the production and consumption of newspapers, broadsides, pamphlets, legal documents, and books, the republican ideology of print arranged the values of generality over those of the personal. In this cognitive vocabulary the social diffusion of printed artifacts took on the investment of the disinterested virtues of the public orientation, as opposed to the corrupting interests and passions of particular and local persons."[18]

Presenting his generalized self replicated in print time and again, Franklin exemplifies the ideology that disembodied him. The personal self was not to be written and was not even to be spoken in public. Indeed, so guarded was personality that for Franklin to write was, in effect, to publish even if print were not the goal, and he regarded all writing as public property.

Thus, in justifying the publication of some confidential letters written by Governor Thomas Hutchinson that he had obtained, Franklin coolly stated, "It is in vain to say, this would be betraying private Correspondence, since if the Truth only was written, no Man

need be ashamed or afraid of its being known; and if Falshoods
have been maliciously covered under the Cloak of Confidence, 'tis
perfectly just the incendiary Writers should be exposed and punished."[19] There may well be more than a touch of sophistry in this
argument that nothing should be written, even in confidence, unless
it can bear public exposure; that, in effect, there is no such thing as
private correspondence. The contention reminds us that Franklin
was the first American printer of *Pamela*, the work that set the style
for the age's popular epistolary novels, revelations, as it were, of
private correspondence, and it also leads to second thoughts about
the way Franklin may have viewed the opportunities he received
as postmaster. For him, to write was to publish.

Carried to a logical extreme, such a contention means that there
is no such thing as intellectual property. Once a person commits
ideas to writing they become the legitimate possession of all who
can read. Franklin's scientific career proceeded from this premise as
he exchanged theories of electricity with his correspondents or de-
clined to patent his stove because it was designed for all who could
read about its merits. He even, notoriously, applied it to dismiss
plagiarism in a manner that must have warmed the heart of Stephen
Burroughs if he learned of it. Disdainful of the doctrinal preaching
of his day as socially inconsequential at best and socially divisive
at worst, Franklin remained apart from sectarian controversy, a
Presbyterian in name and a Deist in belief. But when Samuel Hemphill, a Presbyterian minister from Ireland, appeared in Philadelphia,
Franklin, impressed by his "most excellent discourses," became his
zealous partisan in the controversy that arose after Hemphill's moral
preachings were accused of heterodoxy because they stressed good
works rather than piety. To the chagrin of the Hemphill party,
however, the case against their man was suddenly strengthened
beyond appeal by the discovery that without acknowledging the
fact he had preached sermons by others that he had memorized.
Although the Hemphill party disintegrated as a result, Franklin

wrote, "I stuck by him, however, as I rather approv'd his giving us good Sermons compos'd by others, than bad ones of his own Manufacture."[20] For him ideas were general property and their consequences rather than their origins were what counted.

The argument that maintains the publicity of writing implies the legitimacy of secrecy in all matters kept from print. Conduct that is not on public display and speech that is not overheard have no obligation to be consistent with what comes under public view. The taciturnity of the personal is, for Franklin, the logical complement of the publicity of the general.

"Oratory in this age?" Adams exclaimed in disgust at its decline. "Secrecy! Cunning! Silence! *voila les grandes sciences des temps modernes.* Washington! Franklin! Eternal silence! impenetrable secrecy! deep cunning! These are the talents and virtues which are triumphant in these days." And he thought he knew the reason:

> Silence is most commonly design and intrigue. In Franklin it was very remarkable, because he was naturally a great talker. I have conversed with him frequently in his garrulous humors, and his grandson, Billy, has told me that he never knew a greater talker than his grandfather. But at other times he was as silent as midnight, and often upon occasions and in relation to subjects on which it was his duty to speak. Arthur Lee told me he had known him to sit whole evenings in London, without uttering a word, in company with the first men for science and literature, when the conversation had turned upon subjects on which he was supposed to be well informed.
>
> Whether the age of oratory will ever return I know not. At present it seems to be of little use, for every man in our public assemblies will vote with his party, and his nose is counted before his seat.[21]

While the rise of parties diminished the consequences of oratory in legislative assemblies, it augmented the consequences of print because of the press's role in influencing voters to elect members of one or another party. Thomas Green Fessenden, the feisty poet of Federalist doggerel, scolded his party for "not taking pains to circulate anti-jacobin newspapers, and other periodicals, as antidotes to the poison of the Aurora, the Democratic Press, the Chronicle &c. It is folly to say that exertions of that kind will have no effect. Our adversaries ought to have taught us better. Their maxim is command the press and we command the union."[22] Fessenden, however, underestimated the avidity with which his party seized the lesson. As Gordon Wood demonstrates, the Federalists not only counterattacked in presses they controlled but did so with maxims about representational government and the popular character of the Constitution that were similar in kind to the slogans of their opposition. "By using the most popular and democratic rhetoric available to explain and justify their aristocratic system," Wood observes, "the Federalists helped to foreclose the development of an American intellectual tradition in which differing ideas of politics would be intimately and genuinely related to differing social interests." The result was the creation of "that encompassing liberal tradition which has mitigated and often obscured the real social antagonisms of American politics."[23]

The establishment of the United States and the spread of print went hand in hand. The Constitution itself was a printed document;[24] written by "We the people" it was authored by no particular person but anchored in the fiction of the general made possible by print, and it was not signed by individuals in their own right but by representatives of the people of each state. The press's role in influencing elections compelled both parties to employ similar rhetorical appeals in their effort to attract the voters. The "liberal tradition" which Wood identifies was not the result of a liberal press but of the fact that the press by its very nature shaped itself to the widest possible audience and, therefore, regardless of party repeated the catchwords that had emerged as icons in the Revolution.

As the spread of the press was linked to both the spread of

personal as opposed to real property and the shift from immanence to representation in commercial transactions, so it was linked to the issue of political representation. Even the stoutest patriotic opponents of the argument that the American colonists were virtually represented by Parliament came, after the Revolution, to see that the notion of literal representation—of the body of representatives being a replication of the body of the people—was a greater fiction than that of virtual representation. Women and the propertyless, for example, were not replicated in the republic's assemblies; if represented at all they were represented virtually. Replicated representation, however, was the lifeblood of the press which kept the ideology alive by claiming to be the voice of the people even as it promoted the notion that the people were one.

Cathy N. Davidson has argued that the American novels of the period represent the concerns of precisely those people who were not literally represented politically, particularly women.[25] This contention, however, needs to be located within the larger circumstance that even those who were represented politically were dependent upon literary representation for their sense of their common identity. Print made Americans who were separated by geographical distances, who belonged to different churches, and who came from contrasting social backgrounds aware of the size and nature of the invisible political community to which they belonged, aware, that is, of their power. As Franklin's career illustrates in the strongest light, the immanent world of secrecy could be mastered by the represented world of print.

CHAPTER SIX

MAKING HISTORY

Adams, Jefferson, Rush: Autobiography and the Corruption of History—
The Declaration of Independence and Personality—Franklin and
Representative Autobiography—Rousseau, Emerson, and the
Return of the Immanent

A S the leaders of the revolutionary generation went into retirement, their thoughts turned more frequently to their memory of the events in which they had played an influential role than to news of the current state of the world. In their contemplations, they were struck by the discrepancy between what they believed they had experienced and the accounts of that experience that were crystallizing in the histories and biographies that were beginning to appear. The published versions of their activities diverged widely from their own sense of what had happened. They became all too wryly aware that the most difficult displacement age compelled them to endure was not the yielding of power to the young but the yielding of their experiences to the histories that recounted them. The sad truth age seemed to bring was that the price one paid for making history was that history then made one over in its image regardless of the actuality one had lived.

After surveying the histories then available, Thomas Jefferson wrote to John Adams in 1815:

> On the subject of the history of the American revolution, you ask
> who shall write it? Who can write it? And who ever will be able
> to write it? Nobody, except merely its external facts. All its councils,
> designs, and discussions having been conducted by Congress with
> closed doors, and no member, as far as I know, having even made
> notes of them, these which are the life and soul of history must for
> ever be unknown.[1]

His concern was disinterested, perhaps because whatever the shortcomings of evidence about what had transpired behind closed doors
in Philadelphia in 1776, one "external fact" that was well established
was that Thomas Jefferson had written the Declaration of Independence. The recognition of this fact alone secured him an honored
place in history regardless of misrepresentations or omissions in
accounts of his other achievements.

Adams, on the other hand, was acutely conscious that although
he had had a long and enormously consequential political career,
he had participated in no single momentous event in quite so prominent a fashion as had Jefferson when he wrote the Declaration. He
recognized, moreover, that the historical imagination was more readily drawn to a dramatic setting than to the tracing of ideas. Whatever
had happened behind closed doors in Philadelphia, it had eventuated
in fifty-six provincial gentlemen setting an empire at defiance and
for want of other authority pledging their own lives, fortunes, and
honor. The theatrical moment was so intense that thirty-five years
later Benjamin Rush could still recall "the pensive and awful silence
which pervaded the house when we were called up, one after another, to the table of the President of Congress to subscribe to what
was believed by many at that time, to be our own death warrants."[2]
That was the kind of event that fixed itself indelibly in the historical
imagination, and Adams discovered a phrase for it in a letter he
received from Rush in 1805. Reporting a conversation he had had
with Jean-Victor-Marie Moreau, the French general exiled in the
United States, Rush wrote that Moreau told him that after the Battle

of Marengo he had asked Napoleon why he had chosen the frozen St. Bernard route for his army when he could have followed a more direct and less dangerous road. "It was the scenery of the business," Napoleon answered. "I thought its boldness would have a good effect" (Rush, *Letters,* 2:905).

Adams received the anecdote enthusiastically. He replied to Rush:

> I admire Bonaparte's expression "The Scenery of the Business." The scenery has often if not commonly in all the business of human life, at least the public life, more effect than the characters of the dramatis personae or the ingenuity of the plot. Recollect within your own times. What but the scenery did this? or that? or the other? Was there ever a *coup de théâtre* that had so great an effect as Jefferson's penmanship of the Declaration of Independence? . . . I have a great mind to write a book on "The Scenery of the Business."[3]

Despite the fact that he had been active in the cause of independence for some years before Jefferson, who, indeed, had been a member of Congress for scarcely a year when he wrote the Declaration—and a relatively silent member at that—nothing in Adams's career had been so surrounded by the scenery of the business. In addition to having been, as he believed (with some justification), underestimated he had also, thanks in good part to the advent of the party system and the vigorous polemical use his opposition made of the press, been insulted and slandered with unabashed blatancy.

When Adams commented upon history, then, he did so with an understandable touchiness about its treatment of him. But beyond such self-concern, he and his distinguished correspondents, Jefferson and Rush, were also fascinated by the phenomenon of fame itself.[4] Raised under monarchical government in which fame attached itself principally to birth and prowess in arms, and schooled in the classics where fame in addition attached itself to genius, these lads from

Boston, Philadelphia, and rural Virginia had had no experience that could have led them to anticipate fame for themselves beyond the local. The twenty-one-year-old Adams, teaching school in Worcester, wrote of fame, for example, as something in a world apart from his. Even as he hungered for it he also consoled himself for the impossibility of his ever attaining it by telling his diary that those who love fame "descend to as mean tricks and artifices, in pursuit of Honour or Reputation, as the Miser descends to, in the pursuit of Gold. The greatest men have been the most envious, malicious, and revengeful." Only one American at that time, a "Mr. Franklin of Phyladelphia," had achieved fame; he possessed "a prodigious Genius cultivated with prodigious industry."[5] As for himself, Adams felt as he entered upon the practice of the law that to pursue fame would be to indulge his vanity, which, ironically, could draw him into fopperies that would damage his reputation. And it was reputation, not fame, that brought clients (*Autobiography,* 1:78).

Yet with the success of the American Revolution and the founding of the republic fame came to Adams and his fellows, and with it came the misrepresentations of history. When in their retirement they contemplated what was being written about their times, beyond their understandable if doomed concern that they be represented accurately they were absorbed by the way fame was won or lost in the published histories rather than the event. In April 1809 Rush wrote to Adams:

> A reverence for religion and a regard for truth, liberty, family honor, and the interests of society may make it indispensably necessary for a man who has been wronged by the country or the age in which he has lived to appeal to the world at large and to posterity for the acquittal of the follies or crimes with which he has been charged. Knowing that you feel your obligation to all these objects, and your desire to maintain a fair and just character, I have formerly suggested to you to employ the evening of your life in writing "the history of your own times" as far as you were an actor in them.

Let them be published by your sons after your death. It will be more than a patent of nobility to your descendants to the end of time. (*Spur of Fame*, p. 141)

And Adams in turn charged Rush with a related task:

Dr. Rush! I request you or your son Richard to write a treatise or at least an essay on the causes of the corruption of tradition and consequently of the corruption of history. For myself, I do believe that both tradition and history are already corrupted in America as much as ever they were in the four or five first centuries of Christianity, and as much as they ever were in any age or country in the whole history of mankind. (*Spur of Fame*, p. 186)

Paralleling the new political dispensation established by his generation with the new spiritual dispensation established by Jesus, Adams thought it had undergone a degradation far swifter than the corruption which overtook the Christian church, and to this speedy decay of principle he attributed the mendacity of history. With social glory placed beyond reach by the contentious partisanship of those who wrote history, personal honor alone could be salvaged. The preservation of a good name was to be a family matter: Adams's sons, says Rush, should publish their father's memoirs, and Rush's son, says Adams, might collaborate in his father's treatise.

Neither Rush nor his son composed that treatise on the corruption of history. But in 1800 Rush had already commenced his autobiography, the kind he later recommended to Adams, who, indeed, did not need the urging since three years before Rush's suggestion he had already begun his autobiography. Then, in 1821, Jefferson also found reason to begin making extended notes on his life. In each of these cases regardless of other motives the autobiographer was responding to a sense that the published histories were so untrue to his experience that even though there was no way to counter such misrepresentations publicly he should do what he could toward leaving a written record that would at least inform his family privately of the truth of what had happened as he had participated in it. Taken together these autobiographies, fragmentary as they are, do not form the treatise on the corruption of history that Adams called for, but they do provide a lively commentary on that theme by means of contrastive illustration as each writer offers his assessment of the motives of other actors as well as his own and in general attends to the more private dimensions of experience that escaped the printed histories.

Each insisted his was a private document. Rush addressed his "dear children" at the outset, telling them: "My life has been a variegated one. Under a conviction that I shall not live to give its details to the younger branches of my family, I have concluded to put upon paper a few incidents that may perhaps afford entertainment and instruction to them when I am no more. It is my wish that it may not be read out of the circle of my family, and that it may never be published."[6] Jefferson was terser, simply stating that at age seventy-seven he was writing "for my own more ready reference, and for the information of my family."[7] Adams, however, with his highly developed sense of the injuries that report had inflicted upon his name together with his persistent flare for the oratorical opened with an elaborateness that belied the disclaimer he was ostensibly making: "As the lives of Phylosophers, Statesmen or Historians written by them selves have generally been suspected of Vanity, and therefore few people have been able to read them without disgust; there is no reason to expect that any Sketches I may leave of my own Times would be received by the Public with any favour, or read by individuals with much interest." But he did, he said, want to leave for his posterity in his "own hand Writing" proof of the falsehood of the many calumnies against his name. And with a Puritan's insistence upon improving any occasion beyond its evident worth, Adams advised: "It is not for the Public but for my Children that I commit these Memoirs to writing; and to them and their Posterity I recommend, not the public Course, which the times and the Country in which I was born and the Circumstances which surround me compelled me to pursue: but those Moral Sentiments and Sacred Principles, which at all hazards and by every Sacrifice I have endeavored to pursue through Life" (*Autobiography,* 3:253–54).

That each claimed his version of his life was a private document meant only for his family is less a statement of fact than the assumption of a rhetorical position. The kind of record Adams wanted to correct was more public than private; his claim for privacy was based on his disgruntled contention that the public would not rather than should not be interested. Jefferson wrote first for his own and next for his family's reference; no injury would seem to be done to his intent if yet others found his writing useful for their reference. Rush alone pointedly insisted not only that his autobiography was meant for his family but that he wished "it may never be published." And therein lies a paradox because while Adams and Jefferson were less insistent than Rush upon privacy, under its immunity they pulled together notes in an undeveloped fashion. On the other hand, Rush, who insisted upon never being published, prepared the most finished—which is to say publishable—manuscript, and, moreover, included in it character sketches of all but one of the fifty-six signers of the Declaration of Independence, a series of descriptions quite out of place in a life designed to be read only by his family but of enormous value to a public interested in American history. In sum, each of these autobiographies compromises its claim for privacy although all, to be sure, take that intended privacy as a license to be fragmentary, impressionistic, and even careless.

The assumption of writing for the self, and the self's closest extension, immediate heirs, permits each writer to speak of personal motives and of personality in general when accounting for public events. Were he writing publicly, the political ideology in which both he and his American readers participated would have required of him an account in which he depersonalized himself and represented his actions as subordinate to the ideas and circumstances that made the Revolution; represented himself, that is, as a servant of his society. The ideology that replaced the concept of a state embodied in the sovereign with the concept of a state diffused among the people separated personality from public history; the republican acted in representation of the principles of his fellow citizens. But when the autobiographer marked his writing as private, he could introduce his particularized self as the subject of his own and the corrective of public history.

Ironically, the Declaration of Independence that signaled the end of personally embodied government also presented the time's most stirring example of men grounding political action in their immanent selves. Eight years later a constitution written by "the people" was signed by men who thereby indicated the "unanimous consent of the States present" rather than their own persons. But the Declaration had closed with the statement that "for the support of this Declaration, with a firm reliance on the protection of divine Providence, we mutually pledge to each other our Lives, our Fortunes, and our Sacred Honor." With no model of government other than that of the state embodied in persons, as the Great Britain against which they were rebelling was embodied in the king, the signers put their names for their lives. Thereafter immanence was replaced by representation as the folklore of republicanism celebrated the hero who is motivated by ideals untinctured by personal interest.

Benjamin Rush had neither a long nor a prominent political career compared with his friends Adams and Jefferson; his distinction lay outside of government service. But he was a signer of the Declaration of Independence, and when he arrived at that point in his autobiography he made clear that it was the most important moment in his life. He could not say much about his role in the events that led up to the adoption of that document, but in pledging his life when he signed it he had made his life a part of that document. Correspondingly, that document with every life signed into it became part of his life, and his inclusion of the character sketches of the signers in his autobiography was a consistent if extraordinary absorption of the Declaration into self.

Jefferson recognized that his authorship of the Declaration would gain him immortality regardless of whatever slanders, misrepresentations, or infamy political factionalism might visit upon his other achievements. But he must have feared that his fame was vulnerable to the contention that in writing the Declaration he merely acted as amanuensis for a committee, because in his autobiography he not only asserted his authorship of the Declaration but went on to give its text, thus writing it in as a segment of his life. Moreover, he did so in such a way that the reader could compare his version with that revised and adopted by Congress and so note that the adopted document was in all but minor details the work of Thomas Jefferson.

Adams's activity on behalf of independence had a longer history and was more vigorously pursued prior to July 4, 1776, than that of Jefferson, but, as he ruefully recognized, his activity lacked the scenery of the business. Accordingly, in his autobiography he sought to transfer emphasis from the Declaration as a great causal event to the Declaration as the inevitable outcome of the series of events in which he had played an important part. A member of the committee charged with preparing the Declaration, he referred to Jefferson as its penman and stressed the factors that prepared the public to accept the idea of independence. The clear implication was that the Declaration would never have been made were it not for the receptive public mind that he had been instrumental in preparing. The central importance accorded the Declaration in the three autobiographies prompts the conclusion that the combination of personal and public embodied in it provided each writer with the ultimate justification for placing his private history on record.

Rush died in 1813 shortly after achieving his longtime wish to reconcile Adams and Jefferson, who for decades had been estranged by political differences that had been exacerbated into hostility by their respective champions in the press. Their renewed correspon-

dence, Rush accurately foresaw, would amount to a richer commentary on their times and a fuller portrait of the character of an
American statesman than any historian or biographer could supply.

In that correspondence, too, the Declaration occupied a prominent position. One of the first letters Jefferson sent Adams as they
renewed their acquaintance contained the news of Rush's death, and
in it Jefferson subordinated the man to the great event:

> Another of our friends of 76. is gone, my dear Sir, another of the
> Co-signers of the independence of our country. And a better man,
> than Rush, could not have left us, more benevolent, more learned,
> of finer genius, or more honest. We too must go; and that ere long.
> I believe we are under a half dozen at present; I mean the signers
> of the Declaration. (*Adams-Jefferson Letters,* 2:323)

As they corresponded they pursued Adams's interest in the oc-
currences that led to independence, particularly his persistent interest
in who "first" broached the idea—an unanswerable question that
had become an obsession with him—and Jefferson's less insistent
interest in the Declaration's consequences. And they kept a keen
eye on the dwindling list of surviving signers. No longer active
publicly, they were in their private writings enjoying the opportunity
to measure public events against personal experience, and they indulged the lesson of experience that taught that even the most
rational of all forms of civil government, the republic, was built upon
the shifting sands of passion.

When Jefferson wrote in his autobiography of becoming governor of Virginia in 1779, he remarked, "Being now, as it were,
identified with the commonwealth itself, to write my own history
during the first two years of my administration, would be to write
the public history of that portion of the Revolution within this State"
(*Life,* p. 52). As he defined it, he then had no private life at all, and

accordingly he passed over those years in his autobiography. In the more common sense of the phrase, of course, Jefferson continued to have a private life in those years, but for him his "own history" was not the account of his relation with family, friends, or lovers, but rather the account of his political and intellectual pursuits which either did not appear in the public record or which separated him from the course events took. When his private sense of matters was identical with his public performance, as when he was governor, he had no "own history" to record in his autobiography. For Adams and Rush also, the writing of one's own history was necessitated by the wish to correct or supplement public history.

The same cannot be said of Benjamin Franklin, whose *Autobiography,* indeed, stops before it arrives at the period when he became involved in the movement for independence. He did not aim to correct or supplement public history with his account of his life but proceeded from the remarkable perception that in a republican age the history of a common man is the history of his society; that is, that in the new age public history is the story of how citizens combine to effect their ends. Franklin sensed that the very instinct for self-enlargement that motivates the autobiographer is the same as that which motivates the reader. Although the reader may be drawn to the life of another because that other is famous, what finally holds his attention is not an account of unique accomplishment but an account of how such accomplishment grew from the life that he has in common with the writer.

As particularized as was the self he constructed, Franklin nevertheless stressed his representative nature by emphasizing those experiences upon which he could generalize. He was not concerned with his unique qualities; what happened to him was typical, as he recounted it, and so instructive—it could happen to you. Attention was thus paid to the kind of personal details—family disputes, thwarted courtship, betrayed friendship—excluded from the accounts of autobiographers who were self-consciously contributing to a history that was transpiring on a scale far larger than their own lives. With his characteristic identification of truth with utility, the theme Franklin advanced was not of special accomplishments but rather of the way his life illustrated the connection between the habits one worked to develop in youth and the position one occupied in age. Although he dwelt on his own youth in greater detail than did Adams, Rush, or Jefferson, he was less retrospective than were they. They looked back on past events in order to abstract truths about history and human nature. But Franklin's repeated movement from narrative description to practical application does not invite retrospection. Even as he reconstructs his past, his repeated conversion of it into specific lessons for the person reading his words at the moment thrusts his writing forward into a future occupied by his audience.

Relative to the others, Franklin's *Autobiography* is a coherent work consisting of finished units rather than fragments. Although it begins as a private letter to his son, it soon changes into a public document. Franklin underscores this change by including the letters from friends that urged him to continue his project because of the benefit it would confer on a general readership, although there is room to believe that he discerned the public nature of his personal memoirs before he received those letters and they appear more in confirmation of his sense of his work's public consequences than as a cause of it. Adams, Rush, and Jefferson sought to complement history with the immanence that eluded its representations. But Franklin, with his belief that to write is, in effect, to publish, offered the represented self as representative history. As a result, his *Autobiography* more closely resembles a novel than do the recollections of his contemporaries. It centers on the formation of character, on, that is, his construction of a character, rather than on public events; it lets us hear a range of voices and dialects; it dramatizes incidents. In general it conveys the feeling that the writer's delight in literary construction plays as important a part in determining what he elects to represent as does his governing sense of the typical and useful. This is not surprising. In offering the history of the individual moving upward economically and socially and outward geographically as the model story of the American (and, by extension, modern man) Franklin was both responding and contributing to the conditions that were augmenting the size and power of the middle class. Those same conditions promoted the novel, shaping it to tell stories that embodied the imaginative life of this class which was its major audience.

Whereas Adams, Rush, and Jefferson strove to correct myths about the history they had lived with the particulars of their experience, Franklin supplied in the narrative of a single life the myth that codified the experiences and beliefs of his countrymen. At the core of older stories was the fable of the inevitable conditions birth imposed upon maturity, but Franklin's myth spoke of the ability of the individual to determine the self it would become in maturity, an ability dependent not so much upon intelligence or other native gifts as upon the studied acquisition of a set of habits. The premium thus placed on behavior made experience all but coextensive with reality and was at variance with doctrines of an inner reality prior to and determinant of conscious experience—at variance with Puritanism's "oedipal" original sin. Such optimism seemed validated by the economic and social success that met the industrious American regardless of birth. There was, then, good reason to believe that all obstacles to human happiness were accidental features of a malleable world and could be eliminated through conscious effort. As such a refashioned world would modify individual character, so, reflexively, individual efforts to improve character, such as the practice of the "art of virtue," would modify the world. It can be argued that the relentless truth of the oedipal myth was not to be overriden, that it returned to American letters in writers such as Hawthorne who revived the psychology (although not the theology) of original sin. But Franklin's *Autobiography,* which made tangible widely held perceptions of America such as those advanced by Crèvecoeur, persisted as a national myth that challenged such deterministic accounts, and, indeed, when conflict between the two became evident, encouraged the assertion of America being exceptional.

None of the autobiographies discussed above was published in its author's lifetime, and it is ironic that the one written by Benjamin Franklin, an undeniable master of the print medium, had the most tangled publishing history, his text suffering, in one scholar's phrase, an "Odyssean fate."[8] Franklin had supervised the preparation of two fair copies, one of which he sent to Benjamin Vaughan in England and the other to Louis Guillaume le Veillard in France, but he died before he could receive their comments. Both copies disappeared and the first publication of the *Autobiography* (1791) was in French, a translation of part of the copy sent to le Veillard, while the first edition in English (1793) was a translation back from the imperfectly translated and incomplete French edition. Confusion was compounded over the century as William Temple Franklin in 1818 published a fuller edition based on a copy of one of the missing fair copies, but in it "improved" his grandfather's style so that it would meet the standards he thought to prevail; and John Bigelow in 1868 published an edition based on the le Veillard copy which he had discovered and purchased in Paris. The book was popular, and many other editions, all in some degree faulty, were published throughout the century.

Finally, in 1949, modern bibliographical science addressed the problem in Max Farrand's "critical edition," which reconstructed the text on the basis of the le Veillard copy recovered by Bigelow in comparison with those editions that could claim some connection with what was probably Benjamin Vaughan's lost copy. The Farrand version was regarded as authentic until Leonard W. Labaree and his collaborators, preparing their annotated 1964 edition, saw faults in it that they corrected. But this edition was in turn corrected by the "genetic text" of J. A. Leo Lemay and P. M. Zall, published in 1981. Here the matter rests, or, in the light of its history, at least pauses for breath. The common reader whose interest has encouraged the many reprintings of the *Autobiography* over the decades probably would not find the changes from one modern edition to another of much importance—the legend it recounts has been substantially in place since 1818—but if one is interested in what Franklin wrote then one is better off reading just what it is that he did write.

One point that appears to be made by the droll adventures of the Franklin text is that autobiography seemed so vainglorious an undertaking in the early days of the republic that even Franklin, who had radically reconceptualized the relation of the life of the individual to the life of his society, seeing the latter to be as susceptible to influence from the former as it was capable of influencing it, even he, in a hesitation that led to the tangles in the history of his text, paused to receive private reactions before publishing. With his characteristic adeptness at disarming potential criticism by a demonstration of seeming candor, he admitted in his first paragraph that he wrote, among other reasons, in indulgence of "the inclination so natural in old Men, to be talking of themselves and their own past Actions" (Lemay and Zall, p.1) and dissipated whatever objections might yet remain by reminding his audience that unlike those who from politeness had to sit and listen to old men ramble on about their lives, they were readers and so could stop attending without giving offense. Still, even he, having written for publication, and, indeed, knowing no other way of writing, was wary of publication.

Franklin died in 1790. Three years later the *Confessions* of Jean-Jacques Rousseau, who had died in 1778, began appearing in print. There Rousseau wrote:

> I cannot be deceived in what I have felt, nor in that which from sentiment I have done; and to relate this is my chief aim. The real object of my confessions is to communicate an exact knowledge of

what I essentially am and have been in every situation of my life. I have promised the history of my mind, and to write it faithfully I have no need of other aids: to enter into my own heart, as I have hitherto done, will alone be sufficient.[9]

The scope of Rousseau's intent—what he is and has been in every situation, rather than the recounting of the situation itself—is not so much beyond Franklin's powers as it is outside of his conceptual frame. Rousseau, as he says elsewhere in the *Confessions,* wishes to speak "great truths," such being what he would characterize as true and useful for his readers, as opposed to Franklin's rational measure of the true and practical measure of the useful, what might be called little truths that accumulate perhaps into bigger ones but that are not offered as great. Rousseau stands apart, if not in opposition to at least in distinctness from his society, occupying an Olympian vantage from which the largest truths can be uttered, while Franklin is in the midst of his society, his reported experiences always a matter of his dealings with others. Franklin invites his readers to weigh his behavior in terms of its consequences rather than to appreciate his feelings. When he acted wrongly, as, for example, when he fled his contract with his brother, he committed, he says, an "erratum." The word means error but its use in English is confined to errors in writing and especially in printing, the kind of errors that can be corrected in a rewriting or a recasting of type with all damage removed. Franklin's use of the term in the moral sphere exactly parallels its meaning in printing, because for each erratum he notes, he notes also the correction. After his brother's death he helped his brother's family to a livelihood, thus, he says, amending his youthful erratum. The indelible impression on his brother's feelings made by his betrayal (as well, for that matter, as any uncorrectable feeling of guilt he himself may have had) does not enter the field of vision he establishes. It is difficult to exaggerate the parallel between conduct and print that Franklin maintains: both are visible and objective, both are to be evaluated with reference to their public consequences rather than their psychological origins, and both, when corrected, erase previous impressions. What for Rousseau is an essential, indelible self is to Franklin a text in a constant state of emendation.

Rousseau flaunts his independence of an approving public: "To please a multitude is to become nothing more than a mere scribbler." He says, "I have always felt that the profession of letters was illustrious in proportion as it was less a trade" (*Confessions,* 3:89). It is certainly unfair to regard Franklin as one who saw letters as a trade. By trade he was a printer not a writer, and if he wrote pieces to feed his press nevertheless he did not see writing itself as a trade but rather as an indispensable instrument for a republican society's economic, social, and political advancement, an advancement that included the satisfaction of valid desires to be amused as well as enlightened. But neither did he see letters as a profession. Writing was the tool of every member of the republic who had use for it in pursuit of his profession.

Rousseau scorned the multitude from his position in a hierarchical society that located him above the multitude. His independence was dependent upon a social order confident of the stability of its structures and so unthreatened by personal individuality within them. On the other hand, republican society, lacking a stable class structure, afforded individuals the opportunity to rise above their origins but sought stability in the implicit regulation of their conduct through public opinion.

Rousseau's sense of a unique mind true to itself and so true to truth depended upon a disconnection between the power of individual expression and its effect on the social order, as opposed to its effect on individuals within that order. He carried this to its extreme by positing exile as the ideal condition for authorship: "unless an author be a man of intrigue, when he wishes to render his works really useful to any country, he must not compose them within her bounds" (*Confessions,* 3:94).

But for Franklin a central truth of his time and country was the reflexivity of the ways in which the individual and society acted upon one another. So confident was he of the interpenetrability of the two that he converted appearance into reality in a denial of the existence of any state of consciousness that was untranslatable into action. The history of the mind or heart as something apart from its manifestations in action would be for him akin to an assertion such as that of the priority of piety over morality made in the Puritan church from which he had departed. The distinction insisted upon between conduct inspired by grace and conduct regulated by reason was for him a distinction without a difference if the conduct were the same in all its visible effects. He had left the Puritan's reasons for differentiating between inner reality and its manifestations in the everyday world and he never arrived at Rousseau's reasons for valuing the sentiment above the consequences.

The memoirs of Adams, Rush, and Jefferson recognize a difference between the private and the public, between, that is, what kind of discourse they are and what kind history is. Franklin, too, of course, recognizes a difference between public and private, but he relocates it since he believes only the unwritten can remain private. Even in memoirs, then, one presents a public (or representative) self.

All four regarded the material world as separate from the world of mind, with the two spheres in constant action and reaction upon one another. Republican government was based on such a view. To assert that the material world is dependent upon mind, or that the individual is superior to society and feeling superior to reason would, for them, be a denial of the principles on which they had founded a nation.

The Declaration of Independence was remarkable rhetorically because even as it embodied the personal presence of its signers it signaled the arrival of a nation dedicated to the principle of representation. More than sixty years later, this political declaration was supplemented by what has since been widely accepted as America's intellectual declaration of independence in Ralph Waldo Emerson's celebrated lecture "The American Scholar." A parallel can be traced between the 1776 document that proclaimed the end of political dependency upon Britain and the 1838 address that affirmed, "Our day of dependence, our long apprenticeship to the learning of other lands, draws to a close."[10] But the contrast between the two is also striking and perhaps more informative. The kind of independence Emerson declared called for character to assume supremacy over intellect, and the liberation he sought for the American was freedom to pursue individuality apart from the wishes of society, freedom to insulate oneself from one's fellows.

The year after he delivered "The American Scholar," Emerson amplified his insistence upon a return to immanence thus:

> There is no history. There is only biography. The attempt to perpetuate, to fix a thought or principle, fails continually. You can only live for yourself; your action is good only whilst it is alive—while it is in you.... The new individual ... can owe his fathers nothing. There is no history; only biography.[11]

Numbered among those fathers who can be owed nothing are the founding fathers who saw their biographies as subordinate to history. While commonly regarded as a major American literary epoch, the age of Emerson that realized the return of the immanent heralded by Rousseau did not do so without a corresponding loss. As a sure faith in the republic activated the writing of the self as representative, so the perceived failures of the republic promoted the doctrine of literary individualism and the writing of the immanent self, a development that encouraged the removal of the literary into a separate and sometimes adversarial culture.

CHAPTER SEVEN

THE PERSISTING PAST

Thomas Jefferson and Timothy Dwight—Continuity despite Revolution—
Wieland—Irving, Cooper, and Literary Conservatism

O N March 1, 1790, Congress passed an act that required the marshals of the several political districts to "cause the number of the inhabitants within their respective districts to be taken, omitting Indians not taxed, and distinguishing free persons, including those bound to service for a term of years, from all others."[1] Thus was the first census (officially termed an "enumeration") initiated in fulfillment of the constitutional requirement that representatives and direct taxes be apportioned among the states "according to their respective numbers." Additionally, seeking to gain an estimate of the nation's military and industrial strength, Congress also ordered the marshals to distinguish the sex and color of free persons and specify the number of free males over and under the age of sixteen.

Ten years later, the act authorizing the taking of the second census expanded the range of inquiries only slightly when it required the marshals to gather further details of the age distribution of free whites and included females as well as males in that count. Such a charge fell far short of the information requested by the nation's two most prominent men of learning, Thomas Jefferson, president of the American Philosophical Society, and Timothy Dwight, president of the Connecticut Academy of Arts and Sciences. Fiercely opposed to one another in all matters connected with politics, religion, and social life, these formidable exemplars of liberal and conservative thought in their separate petitions had asked that the census takers be instructed to gather the kind of data that offered a basis for social and economic forecasting. They sought information on the birthrate, a more detailed breakdown of the population into age groups, a differentiation between the number of native- and the number of foreign-born, tables of the numbers in each occupation, and a specification of the numbers in each city, town, and county.

What each would have made of such information had it been collected may be confidently conjectured, because at the turn of the century Jefferson, in the ascendant, was welcoming signs of growth and expansion as evidence of the vitality of democracy while Dwight contemplated the approach of anarchy. As president of Yale Dwight had returned his university and Connecticut as a whole to orthodox Calvinism after the heterodox days of the American Revolution, and he stood at the head of an alliance of clerical and social autocrats who strove with success to make Connecticut the fortress of Federalism. A southern student at Dwight's Yale reported:

> The clergy so far from being the meek and lowly followers of Christ
> ... are the most violent partizans, the most busy electioneers, the
> source of violent animosities and discussions and the very essence
> of political wrangling and disturbance! ... Their situation and im-
> portance here gives them an influence but little thought of in states
> southwardly of this. ... They tell their charge that they must vote
> for such and such men to represent them, or their religion and peace
> will be in danger. These very men when elected would naturally
> resound the praises of the clergy and say *they* must be supported.[2]

A historian of Federalism notes that such autocratic assumptions did not so much represent the last stand of an old order as they "marked the first concerted effort on the part of the business and professional class, together with prosperous landowners, to arrogate to themselves direction of the nation's affairs."[3] But in January 1801, the month then reckoned as beginning the new century, that effort seemed a losing one as the republicanism of Thomas Jefferson and the popular appeal of Aaron Burr, Dwight's scapegrace cousin, appeared certain to prevent the reelection of John Adams. When, therefore, Dwight in that month delivered a discourse in which he reviewed the century just past, he seized the occasion to shore up his weakening political cause by providing a brief course in American history as seen through the corrective lenses of Federalism.

The eighteenth century, Dwight said, had been marked by four crucial events. The first three were, in chronological order, the British wresting of the North American empire from the French; the American Revolution followed by the measures taken to correct the depreciation of currency; and the growth and prosperity of New England as evidenced by an increased number of churches and colleges, greater wealth, and an improvement in the general health. As can be seen, Dwight's chronological progression was also a spatial contraction—from empire, to nation, to region—but in his view this indicated an advancement rather than a decline. The highest values of civilization, he believed, could be realized only within a society unified by a common religion and common manners. In New England, Puritanism had formed a people who emphasized the skills of social intercourse, nourished common schools, stimulated moral and economic activity, and acknowledged the great political truth that being free is consistent with being governed. Such a people would remain strong so long as they contained themselves within clear boundaries and avoided expanding to a size that attenuated their identity. Back in the days when he wrote verse, Dwight had penned the line, "Much virtue's found in fencing well."[4]

As an officer of the Crown, Dwight's father had participated in the French wars, the first of the important events of the previous century that Dwight identified. He himself as army chaplain, then

farmer, school teacher, preacher, and college president had participated in the second and third events. But all three were overshadowed, he warned, by the fourth event, which had commenced at
the close of the century and was still unfolding—the fearful outbreak
and spread of infidelity. It had originated in France, promoted by a
culture that in its celebration of reason in art, theater, and fashions
had destroyed religion. Now infidelity was making inroads upon
American society. "Will you send your daughter abroad in the attire
of a female Greek?" Dwight asked in his peroration; "Will you
enthrone a Goddess of Reason before the table of Christ?"[5]

What had been conducted as a reasoned historical analysis cul-
minated in an emotional assault upon infidels who though unnamed
were readily identifiable as those who supported Jefferson: "The
strong sympathy which, unhappily, and on no rational grounds,
prevailed here toward those, who were leaders in the French Revolution, and toward the Revolution itself, prepared us to become
the miserable dupes of their principles and declarations. They were
viewed merely as *human beings, embarked deeply in the glorious cause
of liberty;* and not at all as *infidels,* as the *abettors of falshood,* and the
enemies of Righteousness, of Truth, and of God" (*Discourse on the Last
Century,* 32).

As saint depended upon sinner for a sense of his orthodoxy, so
the society Dwight valued depended upon the sense of a hostile
environment to keep its boundaries marked and its moral muscles
toned. Accordingly, he lamented the relative calm that had descended
upon New England since the Revolution. Enemies were still out
there, to be sure, but, as he observed, they no longer appeared as
such:

> Formerly the energetic government, established in New England,
> together with the prevailing high sense of religion and morals, and
> the continually pressing danger from the French and the savages,
> compelled the inhabitants into habits of regularity and good order
> not surpassed, perhaps in the world. But since the American Rev-

olution, our situation has become less favorable to the existence, as well as to the efficacy of those great means of internal peace. The former exact and decisive energy of the government has been obviously weakened. From our ancient dangers we have been delivered, and the deliverance was a distinguished blessing; but the sense of danger regularly brings with it a strong conviction that safety cannot be preserved without exact order and a ready submission to lawful authority.[6]

That useful sense of danger was, however, unfortunately blunted because, insidiously, "a first feature of Jacobinism is to deny every dangerous doctrine and effort of Jacobins" (*Discourse on the Last Century,* pp. 49–50).

A political philosophy that required danger for its fullest realization and so conjured enemies when they were not present did not have a promising future, and, indeed, it was overwhelmed by the republican philosophy with its receptivity to change and difference. At the same time, however, the backward-looking provincialism that doomed Dwight's political philosophy provided a rich field for the growth of literary culture. Even if he did mistake the manners of New Englanders for a model of national morality, his ideas were, nonetheless, grounded in an existing society and shaped to a known landscape rather than tied to a utopian society and projected onto an unmapped wilderness. While Jefferson's republican polity required tracts of vacant space as the site for its actualization, Dwight's more autocratic polity was derived from the history of an inhabited region. The spatial correlative of the liberal social vision was boundlessness, and its temporal justification was to be provided by the future. The spatial correlative of the conservative social vision was delimited land, and its temporal justification was derived from the past. Dwight said that Jefferson's attitude toward territorial expansion reminded him of the farmer "who once said, that he wished there was no outside row to his corn-field."[7]

Soon after becoming president of Yale in 1795, Dwight entered into the annual practice of making a long journey during the fall recess when the students were freed to help at home with the harvest, and, usually, he also made a shorter journey in the winter. These travels took him as far into New York State as Niagara and to all points in New England from the Canadian line to Long Island Sound, from the Berkshire Hills to Provincetown, from Lake Champlain to Rhode Island. He saw the sights, talked with the citizenry, preached at the churches, visited the schools, and participated in whatever civic rites happened to be occurring at the time of his visit. For some ten years he made these journeys on horseback, and afterward, for as many years, by chaise or sulky, usually accompanied by one or more companions, a son, a colleague from college, a personal friend. Upon his return he would convert the notes he had gathered into an account of what he had seen, and over the years this project swelled into thousands of manuscript pages. On his deathbed in January 1817, Dwight requested that these manuscripts be published; accordingly, under the supervision of his family, the first two volumes of *Travels in New England and New York* came out in 1821, the last two in 1822, and a London edition of the whole in 1823.

The natural and the social history of the places through which he traveled seemed equally to engage Dwight's imagination. He formulated scientific hypotheses about the geology and agronomy of the regions, often traveling with Benjamin Silliman, whom he had appointed to the first professorship of chemistry in any American university, and he collected anecdotes of local history as avidly as he did scientific data. As a consequence, when back home "Pope" Dwight of Connecticut spoke from college lectern or church pulpit, autocratic as his manner may have been, it was, nonetheless, informed by a constantly renewed experience of the society that embodied his ideas.

In contrast, republican idealism separated political truth from error by pursuing reason in abstraction from the prejudices that underpinned existing societies. Such idealism spoke principally of a nation that was to be. Jefferson's *Notes on the State of Virginia* (1787) is no more remarkable for the precision with which he denotes what is known about the parts of his native state that he has seen and for which he possesses factual information than it is for the way in which an irresistible inclination impels his thoughts to travel into the vastness of a west about which he can but speculate.[8] At the time of his writing, Virginia claimed territories amounting to almost a third of the continent, and in contrast to Dwight's culture that maintains definition by fencing well, Jefferson's realizes itself by dispersal.

Contemplating the Louisiana Purchase and the staggering prospect of an interoceanic nation, Dwight said, "People in a great measure ignorant of each other, with no strong feeling of common interest, and separated by a wide distance, naturally have but little sympathy for each other; and the mere fact that they are under one government may not prove a sufficient bond of union" (*President Dwight's Decisions*, p. 73). As a Federalist he supported a strong central government and accordingly saw the acquisition of more land as a further weakening of a nation whose coherence was already stretched to the breaking point: "Are our countrymen strongly attached to those who dwell in distant states? are they much attached to the government of the United States? And if a disregard of the general government has already been extensive, what would it be after a greater extension of the Union?" (*President Dwight's Decisions*, p. 74).

While Jeffersonians were unperturbed by the attenuation of central control consequent upon expansion because they saw union as a political construct, for Dwight the only true union was a people shaped by shared beliefs and habits, not by laws. "We are not going to force people to become republicans," he said when considering the future settlement of the west; "they must act according to their own pleasure in deciding what government they will choose." The corollary was that New Englanders should look to themselves: "I think the motto which was on our old 'coppers' a very good one for us:—'Mind your business.' " (*President Dwight's Decisions,* p. 73).

To his death in 1817, Dwight was able to contemplate with equanimity the probable division of the United States into smaller nations. Should this occur, he felt New England and New York would form a separate country:

> The inhabitants are now substantially one people. Their interests of every kind are inseparably blended, and not a natural or rational cause of division can be found in either their physical or moral circumstances. Should they be separated from their sister states, there cannot be a doubt that their citizens will hereafter find in their local situation, soil, and climate; in their religious and political systems; in manners and morals; in their health, energy, and activity, ample, perhaps peculiar sources of national greatness and prosperity. (*Travels in New England and New York,* 4:373)

Events proved Dwight wrong in his view of the similarities a people must share if they are to constitute a successful political unit. Although severely tested, representative government proved capable of binding people dissimilar in religion, manners, and local circumstances into a union that claimed sometimes to melt such differences and at other times to derive its strength from them. But while political history took this course, the history of American literature was tied far more strongly to Dwight's than to Jefferson's view of what constituted a society. As what came to be regarded as "literary" separated from other forms of written discourse in the new century, such writing drew sustenance from and promoted an America of conserved values rather than an America of expanding democracy. The history of literary culture, that is to say, took a different course from that of political culture although, to be sure, the two were connected. Political culture followed a predominantly liberal course while literary culture, with its sense of darker forces beneath the surface of consciousness and its reliance on the presence of the past as the very essence of narrative, followed a predominantly conservative course.

~~~~~~~~~~~~~~~~~~~~

In the first days of the new nation, enlightened theory envisioned an unbroken continuity from representative government to an unprecedented republican culture. The American Revolution was seen to mark not just one nation's break from its colonial past but the commencement of the modern world. The United States was leading the way into a future in which the human species would realize itself as the one great family it truly was rather than as disparate units divided by separate national interests. While liberty in the ancient world had stemmed from the wild manners of barbaric people and consequently had diminished as civilization encroached upon the savage temper, modern liberty was the offspring of knowledge and so would increasingly strengthen as reason spread and prejudice fled before it.

Among those features of the past that seemed likely to retreat before the expanding light of reason were the arts, since historically they had depended upon the social injustice of a privileged class for their support and upon the irrational for their effects. Even John Adams, far from a democratic ideologue, detected a connection between great art and corrupt power:

> Every one of the fine Arts from the earliest times have been enlisted in the service of Superstition and Despotism. The whole World at this day Gazes with Astonishment at the grossest Fictions because they have been immortalized by the most exquisite Artists, Homer and Milton Phidias and Raphael. The Rabble of the Classic Skies and the Host of Roman Catholic Saints and Angels are still adored in Paint and Marble, and verse.[9]

No one could be certain as to what would replace such art once superstition and despotism had been eliminated, or even if republican society would require any expression other than what was uttered by reasonable people going about their daily affairs freely. In all likelihood, the intellectual culture of an enlightened world would center on the advancement of the sciences and the application of their methods to politics and economy.

Belief in the progress of reason and the growth of knowledge encouraged a flexible mentality that could entertain present doubt or confusion because it was confident of further illumination. Jefferson's is a shining example. After examining and rejecting the three major hypotheses that were meant to account for the fact that seashells had been found at 15,000 feet in the Andes, and yet unable to formulate another, he said, "Ignorance is preferable to error; and he is less remote from the truth who believes nothing, than he who believes what is wrong."[10] This attitude of calm in the face of the unsettled was evinced toward political as well as natural history. In reaction to news of Shays's insurrection, Jefferson famously wrote: "Can history produce an instance of a rebellion as honorably conducted? I say nothing of its motives. They were founded in ignorance, not wickedness. God forbid we should ever be twenty years without a rebellion. The people cannot be all, and always well informed." And if they cannot be well informed, then a rebellion stemming from their ignorance is far preferable to their maintaining the peace through acquiescence in what they think is wrong: "It is a lethargy, the forerunner of death to the public liberty."[11]

Enlightened thought found ignorance preferable to error in science and, correspondingly, rebellion preferable to lethargy in government. The society it projected was ultimately to be purged of prejudice, superstition, and any other motive to action that had not passed the test of reason. And since reason is a universal human possession, each society as it reorganized on rational principles would come to resemble all other societies similarly organized and a universal culture would eventually succeed national cultures. From this viewpoint, those features of American culture that seemed to indicate national inferiority to traditional cultures were actually signs of the international culture of republicanism that was to spread worldwide. What appeared, that is, to be typically American would eventually prove to be not that but typically modern.

Conservative thought, however, measured the society's worth in terms of the worth of the achievements and leadership of the learned class in America. The democratization of American life was eroding such leadership, and praise of uncertainty in thought or restlessness in politics was a sorry rationalization for the increase in the social dominance of the mediocre if not the downright vulgar.

Under the keenly conservative scrutiny of Fisher Ames, some-time congressman, noted orator, and the very model of an American country squire of the old school, American literature in 1800 appeared to be totally undistinguished:

> There is no scarcity of spelling-book makers, and authors of twelve-cent pamphlets; and we have a distinguished few, a sort of literary nobility, whose works have grown up to the dignity and size of an octavo volume. We have many writers who have read, and who have the sense to understand what others have written. But a right perception of the genius of others is not genius; it is a sort of business talent, and will not be wanting where there is much occasion for its exercise. Nobody will pretend that the Americans are a stupid race; nobody will deny that we justly boast of many able men, and exceedingly useful publications. But has our country produced one great original work of genius?[12]

After saying which, Ames proceeded to demolish any hope for the future based on the claim that Greece's literary eminence stemmed from the political liberty of her states: "But Homer and Hesiod, to say nothing of Linus, Orpheus, Musaeus, and many others wrote while kings governed those states. Anacreon and Simonides flourished in the court of Pisistratus, who had overthrown the democracy of Athens. Nor, we may add in corroboration, did Roman genius flourish till the republic fell" (*Works,* 1:25).

Since the form of government in these and other nations he went on to cite had so strong an influence on literary culture, it was clear, Ames said, that American literature would remain inferior so long as the United States remained a democracy. That, however, would not be for long, he predicted. All signs indicated that either the democratic excesses already evident in the nation would result in the collapse of liberty, or the augmentation of wealth would result in a nation of "many poor and a few rich, many grossly ignorant, a considerable number learned, and a few eminently learned" (*Works,* 1:37). In the latter event, luxury would arise and with it a literary culture.

Although diametrically opposed to Ames's political views, radical thought proceeded from a similar perception of American literature as one of "spelling-book makers, and authors of twelve-cent pamphlets," and, also in agreement with Ames, believed such a literature to be the direct result of the political system. But whereas Ames characterized such literature as trivial compared with what he called works of genius, republican enthusiasts were prepared to value it as characteristic of a society of free and equal men who required printed information for their political well-being and economic growth. By traditional aesthetic standards, this was a literature of a very low order indeed, but these standards derived from societies in which oligarchies unjustly imposed their rule on powerless majorities. A republican society governed by the will of the majority would generate a new aesthetic and deem that best in art which best met the needs of the human family as a whole.

In the unsettled days following immediately after the American Revolution, the war and the resulting independence from Britain seemed to almost all Americans to have broken history into halves. The difference between life before the war and life after the war appeared to overwhelm continuities. But as the new nation adopted a constitution, the economy was stabilized, a confidence in the permanence of the union took hold, and a sense of continuity with the prerevolutionary past emerged. Even as Americans supported their

new government and committed themselves to a political future
without precedents to guide them, many were willing, at moments
eager, to recognize that their communal identity did not after all
suddenly spring up in the wake of their political system but was
more deeply rooted in religious beliefs, patterns of conduct, and
everyday attitudes that preexisted the Revolution and had survived
it. The government of the United States they saw as essential to
their best interests yet as an effect rather than a cause of what
characterized them as a people. Such a view, which had inevitably
to be anchored in regionalism, found greater favor with the more
conservative members of the population. It was also more conducive
to the development of a specifically "literary" national literature
than was the view that emphasized the great scope of the changes
brought about by the Revolution and the need to be open to further
change if the potential of the republic were to be realized. A "national" literature, ironically, was dependent for its realization on a
rooted sense of region while the outlook that promoted national
unity through the sharing of political ideals lacked an attachment
to the prerational that is the condition of imaginative literature.

The theme and patterns that recur in the rambling and episodic
accounts heaped up in Timothy Dwight's *Travels* reflect the affinity
existing between his social outlook and the requirements of belles
lettres. This is not to say that the *Travels* is a notable work of belles
lettres, but, rather, that it is a remarkable exposition of the climate
belles lettres require for their nurture.

A good number of the tales Dwight records in his volumes
concern incidents of the revolutionary war. He relates each as it is
prompted by his visit to one or another locale in which the events
took place rather than in relation to any thesis about the war. They
are units in a collection that includes stories of the seventeenth-
century Indian and the eighteenth-century French wars, and they
function as do the observations of climate and geography to furnish
out a description of New England society, because a major theme

of the *Travels* is the continuity of the New England character beneath the shift of events. The Revolution is viewed as a major but not a cataclysmic event. Since Dwight's narratives are subordinated to his aim of describing the stable New England culture he encounters on his journeys, one of its aspects may be illustrated by an anecdote from the Revolution but another by an incident from the Pequot War of 1636. Public events reveal the character of the people rather than alter it.

Despite the chronological frame provided by his journeys, Dwight's volumes are finally oriented spatially rather than temporally; they are verbal mappings of a society in its particular landscape by a social geographer who crisscrosses the terrain he is plotting. Dwight speaks scarcely at all of himself or of his traveling companions. The observer is subordinated to the observed, the historical tales he recounts are subordinated to the scene that calls them up, and the narrative frame of traveling is subordinated to the space that is thus comprehended.

Dwight's sense of a cultural continuity more powerful than political change is attached to his sense of the limits original sin places on human reason. He believed in the mind's powers of discovery and he pursued scientific questions avidly. Under his supervision, as one scholar has noted, "Yale pioneered in its offering of chemistry, mineralogy, and geology, far in advance of the rest of the country."[13] We find him in Jefferson's company petitioning Congress to gather data that will enable scientific social planning, and the descriptive intent of his *Travels* makes it generically closer to Jefferson's *Notes* than to most other travel literature. Finally, however, for Dwight there was a body of knowledge fundamental to a fully conscious human existence that was beyond the reach of rational inference. It was acquired through belief in the word of God as revealed in the Bible transmitted in Christian churches. Such belief was at the root of the institutions and social practices of the New England culture he described. As original sin precedes the growth of reason and determines its limits, a society's shared beliefs and practices precede rational regulations and determine their limits. Hence the presence of histories, legends, and anecdotes in the *Travels* even though the controlling method is descriptive. What Dwight is describing has to be understood in terms of the past. Correspondingly, what Jefferson describes has to be understood in terms of its future, so it is not surprising that his *Notes* contains next to no narrative.[14]

The sense of the present's continuity with the past, exemplified by Dwight, is closely tied to his sense of the conscious mind's continuity with unconscious sources of behavior. His sense of the motive power of original sin led him, as it had led his grandfather, Jonathan Edwards, into psychological speculation and a profound respect for the unconscious sources of the imagination. Pondering the question of whether the mind always thinks, which Locke had answered in the negative, Dwight said that although he could not convincingly refute Locke on the matter, nevertheless for several reasons he thought it probable the soul was always thinking. "It is often the case," he said, "that when we are about to speak, we forget what we were going to say. Is it not easy then to forget when we are asleep; and may it not be that we have many dreams which we never remember?" And further to the point he added, "The imagination is undoubtedly stronger during sleep than when we are awake" (*President Dwight's Decisions,* pp. 33, 36). On the other hand, the view that the present had been severed from the past—that the Revolution marked the beginning of a distinctively new era of liberty founded on reason—was also one that minimized the force of the irrational and in so doing closed off the imagination from its subterranean sources and required it to furnish itself from the well-lit objects that addressed the senses.

———

Charles Brockden Brown's remarkable novel *Wieland* (1798) offers a striking example of the contrasting pull of the day's liberal social theory and the conservative commitments of literary culture. Set in the countryside near Philadelphia in the period before the Revolution, the novel is so intensely concerned with the personal events in the lives of its central characters that its relation to actual historical events, its simple mirroring of the doings of its days, is negligible. But although the novel is unconcerned with the Revolution, its exposition seems deliberately to advance the revolutionary belief that independence from the past can be achieved.

The novel's narrator is Clara Wieland, a learned young woman who initially holds enlightened views; for example, she explains to the reader that "the will is the tool of the understanding, which must fashion its conclusions on the notice of the senses."[15] In her brief account of her ancestry, Clara emphasizes the discontinuity between successive generations. Her paternal grandfather was a Saxon nobleman whose family cut off all relations with him when he married a Hamburg merchant's daughter. He then earned a scant livelihood as a poet and composer, and he died young, as did his wife. Their orphaned son was apprenticed to a trader in London, but by the time his apprenticeship ended he had through reading become so thoroughly imbued with the religious principles of the zealous Protestant sect known as the Camisards that he abandoned trade in response to an inner vocation to go to America to convert the Indians.[16] Once arrived, however, his resolution faltered and he purchased a farm within a few miles of Philadelphia and began to work it. "The cheapness of land," Clara reports, "and the service of African slaves...gave him who was poor in Europe all the advantages of wealth" (*Wieland,* p. 11). Like Crèvecoeur's farmer, the elder Wieland prospered in reflection of the new land's capacity to rehabilitate its settlers, but in his case material advancement failed to prevent a psychological relapse. In the leisure time afforded by his affluence he was revisited by religious ideas, belatedly began a missionary effort that was defeated by both the rebuffs of the Indians and the depravity of his fellow citizens, and returned home to lapse into a melancholia which ended in his being consumed in a sudden and mysterious fire—perhaps spontaneous combustion, perhaps a divine visitation, perhaps yet otherwise caused. A few months later his wife died and six-year-old Clara and her brother were orphans.

Before the plot of *Wieland* unfolds, then, the series of social changes (noble, merchant, artist, farmer), geographical shifts (Germany, England, America), and financial reversals (comfort, subsistence, prosperity) that precede it suggests that the story of the present generation, Clara and Theodore Wieland's, may well be as independent of their father's story as his was from his father's, and his father's was from his father's. And, indeed, so it begins. Whereas their father had for a good part of his life labored, they were at leisure, and whereas their parent was ridden by irrational anxieties and guilts, their guardian had seen them educated in accordance with modern principles. Clara says:

> We were left to the guidance of our own understanding, and the casual impressions which society might make upon us. . . . It must not be supposed we were without religion, but with us it was the product of lively feelings, excited by reflection on our own happiness, and by the grandeur of external nature. We sought not a basis for our faith, in the weighing of proofs, and the dissection of creeds. (*Wieland,* p. 24)

Away from the corruptions of the city and freed from the coarsening effects of labor, Clara and Theodore's upbringing seems to insure that their moral decisions will proceed rationally from understandings furnished with the impressions received by unspoiled senses.

When they come of age, the sister and brother divide their father's property and reside near one another. He marries Catharine and becomes a father while Clara is attracted to Catharine's brother, Pleyel. Rural, rational, and youthful—the little society of the Wielands is peopled by those their age and younger but with no one older—the community at the center of the novel, like the young nation of republican ideals, is freed from the past, confident of the future, and convinced that life lived close to nature affords no entry for vice.

In his maturity, however, Theodore becomes attracted to the doctrine of original sin and is convinced that his reading in Latin writers, in history, and in metaphysics supports it. Despite his modern education, he differs from the rational Pleyel. "Moral necessity and calvinistic inspiration," Clara says, "were the props on which my brother thought proper to repose. Pleyel was the champion of intellectual liberty and rejected all guidance but that of his reason" (*Wieland*, p. 28).

The two pairs of sisters and brothers, however, share so many intellectual and sentimental interests that they are keenly defined in contradistinction to the world beyond the boundaries of their enclave. The difference in religion between Theodore and the others is dealt with amicably until a stranger intrudes into their little society and precipitates a chain of events that convert Theodore's belief in natural depravity into depraved action. As he is increasingly controlled by an inner voice, his temperamental resemblance to his morbidly religious father asserts itself with far more horrible consequences than the fire that consumed the parent. Imagining he is summoned by God to sacrifice his family, he murders wife, children, and ward, and narrowly misses murdering Clara before he is apprehended. Thus, in *Wieland* the past proves inescapable despite the countervailing exertions of natural sensibility, reason, and good will. The dead father gains control of his son; a supernatural inclination of the mind determines the direction of the will. Clara and Pleyel escape the multiple deaths with which the novel closes, but their lives too are wrecked as they not only lose those they love but are unable to account for the cause of these catastrophes in terms of the enlightened beliefs they had held. In the end, significantly, they flee to Europe.

During the course of the novel, Clara moves from her commitment to the idea that the will is the tool of the understanding to the belief that "ideas exist in our minds that can be accounted for by no established laws" (*Wieland,* p. 99). She does so because she increasingly associates her waking thoughts with the images in her dreams. One sequence, for example, links waking thoughts of her father to a dream she had of her brother beckoning her to join him on the farther side of a pit. The sequence culminates in her rising from bed and entering the closet of her bedchamber at night in order to fetch the memoirs of her father, which she wishes to return to bed to read, only to discover hiding in her closet a man whom she first believes to be her brother. He is Carwin, a new member of the Wieland social circle and still very much a mysterious stranger. Although far from handsome, his physical presence is magnetic and Clara recognizes she is attracted to him even as she longs for Pleyel to propose marriage to her. With his concealed past, his habit of lurking unseen on the periphery, and his powers of ventriloquism— an ability, that is, to mislead the senses—Carwin is emblematic of the subconscious mind. Clara's encounter with him as she was about to clarify her feelings by consulting her father's writings blends waking thoughts with the images that occur during sleep as constituents of the imaginative act.

Wieland was the first of four fairly long novels published within two years of one another (1798–99). It appears that for Brown, who wrote with both speed and intensity, the process of composition was the process of discovery; he found what he was going to say only when he was saying it. Like his central characters, he followed the ideas and images prompted by the subconscious mind, and his novels, like the characters' narratives they contain, are attempts of the conscious mind to impose order on a sequence that was not rationally organized in the happening. The terms and tone with which Clara Wieland commences suggest that the Jeffersonian author set out to write a narrative of new beginnings. Plot complication was to come from the effects of ventriloquism on those ignorant of the phenomenon so that they are led to suspect one another since they are unable to distrust their senses. In their confusion they might either seize upon a supernatural explanation for their predicament or insist that although they had not yet discovered it a natural explanation must exist. They could, that is, elect either error or ignorance, and those who kept open minds would finally arrive at a rational explanation.

As events unfolded, however, which is to say as Brown from day to day pursued the logic of the psyche, rational explanation proved to be inadequate. It is true that the baffling phenomenon of the disembodied voices is accounted for scientifically through an explanation of ventriloquism. But by the time explanation arrives it is inadequate to account for the inner voices that Theodore hears and conflates with the voices heard by the outer ear. In the writing of *Wieland,* Brown discovered the power of the subconscious mind and the subsequent limits of reason. Its correlatives were a recognition of the past's hold on the present and of narrative's dependence upon generational continuities. *Wieland* disproved the premises upon which it was begun.

As it happens, Brown himself abandoned his Jeffersonian ideals at about the same time in his short life—he died before he was forty—that he abandoned the writing of fiction. He continued to write nonfiction and did so in good part as a polemicist on behalf of Alexander Hamilton's ideas on political economy. It is tempting, therefore, to suggest that Brown's political conversion was brought about by the self-discovery implicit in his mode of fictional composition. This may well have been the case. But it may also be argued that had novel writing proved profitable, as it decidedly did not, he would have continued a novelist. Be that as it may, *Wieland* strikingly illustrates the tension between, on one hand, a commitment to narrative fiction—and so to the dependence of the imagination on the subconscious mind and of the present on the past—and, on the other, the premises of liberal, republican theory.

The tension is further illustrated by Brown's immediate successors in the writing of fiction. Unlike Brown, Washington Irving began as a staunch Federalist and in his *Knickerbocker History* (1809) lampooned Jefferson with a relish. Accordingly, when he composed the work that earned him fame, *The Sketch Book* (1819–20), he was free from the kind of conflict between political views and literary culture that Brown had experienced some twenty years earlier. His conservative political outlook was entirely in keeping with a literary instinct that sought out antiquated settings and old-fashioned manners for its effects. Although the best-known of his sketches are set in America, the larger number, quite appropriately, are set in England. And even the American sketches insist upon the persistence of the past. So far is the American Revolution from making a distinctive difference in everyday life that it is rendered as an event that, so to speak, did not happen. Rip Van Winkle sleeps through it to awake to changes that fail to disguise the basic similarity between present and past. The man on the horse on the inn's sign may now be labeled Washington rather than King George, but it is the same figure, and those who gather under it are more or less identical with their predecessors of twenty years before. Moreover, while sleeping through the Revolution Rip dreamed a dream of the Dutch discoverers of the Hudson, a dream of founders that calls into question the founding force of the Revolution that it displaces in the narrative.

In contrast to Irving, his major contemporary, James Fenimore Cooper, insisted upon his strong commitment to principles of democracy such as those that informed the policies of Andrew Jackson, and the first novel to earn him fame, *The Spy* (1821), was a novel of the American Revolution. Yet despite the politics he avowed outside the novel's pages, within them Cooper dwelt almost obsessively on the Revolution as a family quarrel conducted by ladies and gentlemen who held substantially the same views of social order and differed only on expediential matters. The plot centers on the members of the upper-class, high-toned Wharton family who are divided by their patriot and loyalist allegiances but who, nevertheless, get along with one another amiably, as, indeed, do the American and British officers in the novel when they meet on neutral ground. While the novel's subtitle, *A Tale of the Neutral Ground,* is a literal reference to Westchester County, New York, which was such a ground for most of the war, the symbolic reference is to the large amount of civilized ground shared by American and British society despite the temporary disagreements that led to war.

The villains of the piece are, on one hand, low-life American irregulars who use the war as an excuse for plundering their social betters, and, on the other, a British officer who attempts seduction through a fake marriage in the shopworn tradition of the seduction novel of an earlier period. If the latter typifies the vices to which aristocratic society is prone, the former are a more menacing warning that America's real problem after the Revolution will not be to curb oligarchy but to reassert the control of the gentleman over the rabble.

Although *The Spy* centers on the Revolution, depicts skirmishes, and even introduces Washington both as a character and an invisible divine presence, it deemphasizes change and celebrates the prewar values that the new nation must conserve. The politics of Cooper's novel thus seem at odds with his explicit political allegiance, and in the face of this both he and many explicators since his time have insisted there is no contradiction because a commitment to political democracy in no way contradicts a belief in social inequality. The contention seems valid enough in the abstract, but since the social rather than the political is the stuff of novels, Cooper's considerable fictional achievement—the world he embodies here, and, most notably, later in the Leatherstocking Tales—constitutes a powerful conservative political statement that overwhelms any nonfictional claims to the contrary.[17]

Novels offer the best illustration of the diverging values of political democracy and literary culture in the early decades of the republic because imperfect as they are they continue to hold a modern reader's attention to a far larger degree than either the poetry or the drama of the period. The one play that seems still to possess some vitality, *The Contrast* by Royall Tyler (1787), further underlines the divergence. The contrast of the title is that between the snobbery and emptyheadedness of Americans who ape European manners and the common sense and sturdy virtue of those attached to plain, republican customs. The hero is an American army officer. Thus, it is to be anticipated that the playwright's theme is that the Revolution does, indeed, begin a new order. But as the play proceeds, the spectator becomes aware that Tyler is also revealing that to the extent that this is so, as he fears it may be, to that extent a native literature, or at least a native drama, will be impossible. The republican hero and heroine whose marriage closes the play are admirable, but as author, spectator, and every other character in the play realize, they are also boring. Although they deserve their happy ending even as the snobs, flirts, and gossips deserve their correction, still a world in which the latter will give way to the former is one in which drama must give way to moral lectures.

The essential disharmony between literary culture and liberal political values has been emblematized by differences between Thomas Jefferson and Timothy Dwight. In their age's terms, both were men of letters, learned in philosophy, natural science, history, politics, and literature, and both in their longest works, *Travels in New England and New York* and *Notes on Virginia,* based their vision of the United States on a description of their native region. The political conservatism of the one and the liberalism of the other is explicit, but more to the present point is that, implicitly, their differing views of the imagination and the scope of reason, their contrasting attitudes toward the presence of the past, and their use or disregard of narrative illustrate literature's dependence upon and unavoidable transmission of conservative values regardless of the author's beliefs.

Literary forms, however, are no more absolute than political beliefs and they shift over time. What was true of the relation of literature to politics in the early national period would not necessarily be true of that relation in a later period. It was clear, though, that if American literature were ever to embody political liberalism, it would not simply be by dint of the author's liberal sentiments. Rather, the conventions of literature itself would have to be radicalized.[18]

CHAPTER EIGHT

CAPTIVE LANGUAGE

Social Science and the Indian—The Lewis and Clark Expedition—

Journal versus History—Language and Captivity

IMOTHY DWIGHT'S parochialism, which led him to believe that the social history of New England contained what most needed to be conserved if America were to remain America, contrasted sharply with Thomas Jefferson's expansiveness, which led him to believe that the natural history of Virginia prefigured the generous conditions that would shape an emerging America. The social dimension of Dwight's Calvinism required individuals to compact themselves into delimited communities in which an implicit standard of group behavior reinforced the order imposed by leaders in church and state. Jefferson, on the other hand, was confident that a decentralized society of cultivators would need little control other than that of the substantial and genuine virtue in the breasts of all who labor in the earth away from the corruptions of the city. But their common interest in science—an essential component of their identity as men of letters—contributed to a similarity in their view of the nature of American nature. According to European science's depreciatory account, the American versions were inferior to the European in all species of fauna and flora common to both continents. The implication was that human life would suffer a corresponding diminution. To set the record straight on American nature, therefore, was a political as well as a scientific duty because to do so was to provide American society with a setting commensurate with its claims for superiority.

Descriptions such as that of Virginia's Natural Bridge in Jefferson's *Notes* or Niagara Falls in Dwight's *Travels* implied the ennobling effect these splendors would have on the lives of those who lived amidst such grandeur, even as statistics on the true size of American animals and plants suggested the generous dimensions of the children who would grow up in America.

But although these observations carried some conviction with regard to the moral and physical makeup of the American, the issue those who championed American nature as a complementary setting for a superior society had most importantly to face was that posed by the Indians, whose way of life had been shaped by the American environment. Accustomed to a historical linkage between rapine in savage warfare and rape, European men of letters puzzled over reports that the Indians although ferociously bellicose were also sexually chaste, even, it was suspected, impotent. The Comte de Buffon, whose depictions of American nature were addressed at length in Jefferson's *Notes,* conjectured that Indian sexual conduct was connected to the absence of large, ferocious beasts, and the Abbé Raynal pitied the Indian weakness in what he called the "prime instinct, prime knot of society."[1] Condemned as antisocial because of their wars, the Indians were also condemned as antisocial because of their sexual restraint. American natural philosophers such as Jefferson and Dwight recognized that their defense of their native continent required an interpretation of Indian life that accounted for their sexual behavior in terms compatible with their being social creatures.

"If a young man were to discover a fondness for women before he had been to war," Jefferson was told by Charles Thomson, secretary of the Continental Congress and a close observer of Indian life, "he would become the contempt of the men, and the scorn and ridicule of the women. Or were he to indulge himself with a captive taken in war, and much more were he to offer violence in order to gratify his lust, he would incur indelible disgrace. The seeming frigidity of the man, therefore, is the effect of manners, and not a defect of nature."[2]

Dwight concurred. The old sachems, he said, counsel the young warriors against giving in to sexual passion since it will make them like women and unfit them for the hunt. Sexual continence is not the result of a "frosty insensibility of constitution."[3]

Similarly, both contended that what was taken to be the natural savagery of the Indian was actually the manifestation of a nurtured character trait. The fearless warrior was an important part but not the whole of his society. Jefferson maintained that the telling difference between Indian and European society was not that between savagery and civilization but rather that between a civilization without letters and one with them. The Indians were like the ancient Romans in their stoic bearing, their bravery in war, and their powerful oratory. "I may challenge the whole orations of Demosthenes and Cicero, and of any more eminent orator, if Europe has furnished any more eminent, to produce a single passage superior to the speech of Logan, a Mingo chief," he wrote (*Notes,* p. 65), and he then put that speech into his text as evidence.

With perhaps a fuller knowledge of Indian life, derived from his travels and his wide acquaintanceship with missionaries, Dwight was more detailed in his account of the civilized behavior of Indians, centering especially upon the Iroquois, a favorite subject of those who valued Indian life most when they perceived it to mirror European institutions: "In their harmony, the unity of their operations, the energy of their enterprises, and the strength and sublimity of their eloquence, they may be fairly contrasted with the Greeks." Although Dwight scorned the idea that the Indians provided a model of the perfection mankind could achieve when restored to nature, he wryly observed that their undoctrinal paganism made them more reliable as neighbors than were contemporary Europeans who wor-shipped reason. "The treaties of the Indians," he said, "though imperfectly observed, were better kept than those of the modern French. . . . Upon the whole they exhibited the general depravity of human nature under all the disadvantages of a profound ignorance but without the peculiar mischiefs of an absurd philosophy" (*Travels*, 4:147–48).

In their contention that the Indians were to be understood as one would understand another civilization, Jefferson and Dwight were representative of an American intellectual community inter-ested in scientific accuracy and anxious about the international rep-utation of their country. A larger number of their countrymen, however, found it to their advantage to maintain a belief in the indelibility of Indian savagery. To say that Indians were both un-civilized and uncivilizable was to justify the violation of their lives and lands. The political and social history of the westward movement of Americans in the nineteenth century illustrates the costly triumph of this view. But, ironically, the countering view of the Indian as civilized led to an intellectual dispossession and subjugation of Indian life that paralleled and even to some extent preceded the physical appropriations being made along the advancing frontier of American settlement.[4] Although the intent may be respect for its integrity, the translation into letters of civilization without letters is the incor-poration of that civilization into the civilization of the translation. The history of the idea of the civilized Indian is the history of his annihilation through letters even as the history of the idea of the savage Indian is the history of his annihilation through physical force.

~eeeeeeeQ)))))eee~

Jefferson was interested in the ample traces of a previous Indian occupancy of land he owned, and even supervised the excavation of an Indian mound on his property. Yet he could write, "I know of no such thing existing as an Indian monument: for I would not honour with that name arrow points, stone hatchets, stone pipes, and half shapen images" (*Notes,* pp. 99–100). With a classically informed sense of what constituted a monument, he understandably found the remains of everyday life to fall short of that standard. Indian culture not only failed to leave a record of its presence through letters but failed to leave it through created objects that stood on a scale with and in contrast to nature. As oratory, the great Indian art, died with the orator, so the objects of everyday living such as hatchets and pipes ceased to speak when they had lost their employers. Unlike the ancient civilizations of Greece and Rome that influenced posterity through their writings and their monumental remains, Indian civilization, in Jefferson's view, survived only so long as there were Indians living it.

Moreover, although Indian tribes maintained a vigorous existence across the continent, despite endangered circumstances along the eastern seaboard, Jefferson appears to have been so convinced that their culture was doomed to extinction that, consciously or not, he treated them philosophically as if they were already extinct. His scholarly interest was not attached to supporting or preserving their way of life but rather to recovering from them all that could be recovered about their origins before they ceased to be available to provide the evidence. The best proof of their descent would come, he believed, from a comparative philological analysis, and so he wrote, "It is to be lamented then, very much to be lamented, that we have suffered so many of the Indian tribes already to extinguish, without our having previously collected and deposited in the records of literature, the general rudiments at least of the language they spoke" (*Notes,* 104). He appeared to accept Indian extinction as inevitable and so felt the learned world had to salvage what it could before the ruin became total. Literature would provide the Indians with the monument they were unable to build for themselves.

In a parallel manner, when Jefferson praised Indian oratory it was ominously appropriate that the theme of the specimen he offered was a lament for the disappearance of the orator's family and tribe, a text that became the standard expression of the Indians as a vanishing people. Oratory is an art of immanence; to represent it in writing is also to erase it. Hence what fitter topic for the orator in such a representation than his own annihilation? In it the Indian himself implicitly acknowledged he could continue living only in the white man's representation of him.

In conscious political practice, of course, Jefferson did not work toward the annihilation of the Indians. As president he pursued a policy he believed would support them. But philosophically his assertion that they left no monuments conveniently complemented his belief that the Declaration of Independence had begun American society anew. Absence of Indian monuments was yet another proof of America's freedom from the past. The natural as well as the political landscape was wiped clean and made available for whatever the new Americans willed.

Although Dwight shared with Jefferson a general view of Indian life as a culture, with his belief in innate depravity and the determining power of the past he differed from Jefferson about the way to recover the origin of the Indians as well as about their probable future. Where Jefferson saw change Dwight saw continuity, and where Jefferson, knowledgable as he was about literature and the arts, inclined toward scientific analyses, Dwight, knowledgable as he was about the sciences, inclined toward literary syntheses, with the Bible providing a model for his practice of perceiving and describing reality in the narrative mode.

Contemplating the question of Indian origins, Dwight fastened on the Indians' own legends as central evidence. Jefferson hoped to reconstruct origins through the science of comparative philology, but Dwight sought to reach the answer through heeding Indian accounts that others dismissed as fairy tales. His biblically grounded theology gave Dwight the sense that faithful interpretation of narrative requires the comprehension of the full sequence of narrated events rather than the skeptical acceptance of only the probable parts. The entire flow of a story has to be regarded if its meaning is to be grasped; truth, that is, resides in the instinct to construct narrative as much as in its content. In defense of Indian myths, Dwight wrote:

> All traditionary accounts which are regularly retained by any nation concerning the place of its origin are almost of course true, i.e., in substance. Those who first communicated them communicated facts. Those who followed have often forgotten some fact and added some fabulous circumstances. But the great and commanding facts have rarely been forgotten, and never mistaken. Those who repeat and those who receive the tradition are here interested in preserving truth, because every nation, particularly every savage nation, considers its origin as honorable to itself and regards it with not a little attachment. The subject also is too simple to perplex the memory and too important to escape it. (*Travels,* 1:88)

Such a view of Indian legends and especially of the irresistible human impulse to derive identity from history led Dwight away from any sense that the Indians were doomed to physical extinction. But he was also convinced they neither would nor should continue to survive by retaining their own way of life, continue to survive, that is, as Indians. Most obviously, he affirmed their need for Christianity, both for the salvation of their souls and because "sin has no tendency to make a happy society; but, among all intelligent beings will always render the social state unhappy in exact proportion to the degree in which it exists" (*Travels,* 3:16). At the same time, in the light of his knowledge of missionary experience, Dwight doubted that Christianity would have much effect on Indian life unless other values central to the culture were first altered. Observing the wretched conditions under which Christianized Indians lived, he recognized there was, in effect, no sound prospect of their becoming orthodox New England Protestants unless they also became, as it were, Yankees, unless, that is, their material as well as their spiritual selves profited. He coolly advised a project of cultural engineering even more deracinating than religious conversion: replace the Indians' love of glory, he urged, with love for property. Thus, although Dwight's literary sensibility led him to recognize in Indian legends an inner life ignored by many another observer, his religious belief held that even the most deeply rooted aspects of identity could be transformed. Accordingly, he advocated conversion of the Indians to the values of the nascent capitalistic society that was advancing upon them.

In their separate ways, then, Jefferson and Dwight countered the vulgar view of Indian savagery with ideas that, in effect, erased Indian culture in the very process of recognizing it. They shared the view that Indian life existed at a primitive stage of human development similar to that from which European civilization had evolved ages ago. Once the modern world burst upon it, therefore, it was doomed to extinction either through physical annihilation or cultural assimilation. Moreover, since Indian life duplicated an early stage in the history of the encroaching civilization it had nothing to offer that the encroaching civilization had not originally possessed and long since modified toward its own ends. To be sure, more than one item of botanic lore, domestic craft, or woodsmanship could be learned from the Indians. But the Indian structure of feeling, the Indian perception of reality, belonged to a world outgrown rather than a world apart, and so no longer contained aught of psychological or intellectual consequence for the new Americans.

Crèvecoeur's farmer exemplified this attitude. Suspended between the horrors of the city dweller's vices and the Indian's savagery and compelled by the war to choose residence with one or the other, he elected the latter. He felt he could better prepare his family for the resumption of agrarian life after the war by temporarily returning them to the conditions that, historically, had preceded farming than by introducing them to the parasitic condition that fed upon it. But since he was acutely conscious that his life among the Indians was a return to an earlier stage of social evolution, he guarded against relapse by governing his family according to a strict code. Even as they lived among the Indians they were to bear in mind that they were superior to them in the literal sense of existing at a higher stage of historical development.

Most obviously, such an attitude was directly opposed to the idea of the noble savage held by Enlightenment theorists and echoed by observers such as William Bartram who shared their optimism. Bartram, for example, said that the Creeks with whom he visited were virtuous by instinct whereas in European society the same moral behavior had to be promoted by compulsions and restraints. "It seems impossible," he wrote, "for them to act out of the common high road to virtue." As a consequence, they are happy in this life: "joy, contentment, love, and friendship without guile or affectation, seems inherent in them, or predominant in their vital principle, for it leaves them but with the last breath of life."[5] Yet Bartram shared with the opposing view of Indian society exemplified by Crèvecoeur the underlying sense that the Indians' way of life was one that civilized peoples had once led and had grown away from. Those such as Crèvecoeur who saw the primitive stage as savage regarded civilization as a process of amelioration of the human condition; those such as Bartram who saw it as instinctively virtuous regarded civilization as a process of recuperation from the damage suffered from the fall out of nature. But whether modern man had arrived there by rising or falling, he was in civilization and the Indian stood outside, either an outgrown version of modern man's primitive self or an idealized model of modern man's irrecoverably lost self. In neither case was the Indian granted an independent presence. As political policy acknowledged the Indians' legal existence only after they surrendered their sovereignty—they could assert their rights to their land only after they recognized that they and that land were subject to the laws of the United States—so literary representation acknowledged the Indians' culture only after they surrendered their history.

～ᴜᴜᴜᴜᴜᴜᴜᴜᴜᴜᴜ～

Jefferson wrote his *Notes* after he had returned to private life from a stormy tenure as governor. Able again to place philosophical interests above political expediency, he projected the disappearance of the Indians, his principal knowledge of them having been gathered from the diminished tribes of the Virginia and Kentucky region.

Some twenty years later, however, President Thomas Jefferson contemplated the trans-Mississippi vastness and its inhabitants with a pressing political need to gather information that would inform national policy. The expedition led by Captains Meriwether Lewis and William Clark was organized to meet this need. Jefferson charged them with describing the shape and content of the enormity that was the American west along the route they were taking from the Mississippi River to the Pacific Ocean, and accordingly, they made maps and collected biological specimens as well as keeping journals and making extensive notes. With regard to the Indians, Jefferson asked the captains to count the numbers of each of the nations through which they passed and note their territorial boundaries, relations with other tribes, languages, traditions, monuments, occupations, domestic arrangements, health, medical practices, laws, customs, articles of commerce, and moral and physical differences from the better-known tribes of the eastern seaboard. When one considers the sheer difficulty of physical survival in so arduous a journey as that they undertook—not just the first white men, but in all probability the first men ever to cross the continent and then recross it—it is truly astounding to realize that they accomplished it with the loss of but one member of the party (who died of fever within the first month), and that while fighting the current of the Missouri for some fifteen hundred miles, climbing into the Rockies on moccasined feet over thorny soil and stony soil, crossing the passes on horses, and descending the Columbia's course by foot and canoe, only to do it all over again in reverse, and while dealing with the psychological stresses that arose from the confrontation of one peril after another, both kept daily journals, drew maps, and otherwise gathered and recorded the information that they were charged with acquiring. When all their documents were finally published in 1904, one hundred years after their setting out, the printed matter ran to eight large volumes.

Although an instrument of the president's philosophical as well as his political interests, officially the Lewis and Clark expedition was a military detachment under the supervision of the secretary of war. Twenty-seven enlisted men together with the two captains were on the military roster, and the addition of York, Clark's Negro slave, and, along the way, a support group of French and mixed-blood hunters and interpreters together with one of their wives, the Indian woman, Sacajawea, brought the total number in the party to forty-five. They started from Camp River Dubois, Illinois, on May 14, 1804, and proceeded up the Missouri during the summer and autumn until they reached the vicinity of the present Bismarck, North Dakota, where they built log huts and wintered among the Mandan Indians. On April 7, 1805, they set out from the Mandan village, proceeded to the headspring of the Jefferson Fork of the Missouri, crossed the Bitterroot range and descended the Columbia to its mouth. Reaching the Pacific coast in November, they housed for the winter in the vicinity of the Clatsop Indians, and on March 23, 1806, began their return. Crossing the Rockies in June, they divided into two parties, one to explore the falls of the Missouri and Maria's River, the other the Yellowstone, both parties reuniting below the mouth of the Yellowstone on August 12, to arrive at St. Louis on September 23, 1806.

In 1814, ten years after the expedition had set out, the *History of the Expedition Under the Command of Captains Lewis and Clark* was published in Philadelphia. The two-volume edition was compiled by Nicholas Biddle at the urging of Clark who, after Lewis's death in 1809, had the responsibility of gaining public awareness of the nature of their accomplishment. The contrast between the daily reality of the expedition led by this frontier-bred Kentuckian and that of the man he persuaded to construct its history was sharp. Biddle is best known today for his presidency of the Second Bank of the United States and his bitter contests with Andrew Jackson over its rechartering, but throughout his young manhood he was known in his native Philadelphia and in literary circles beyond it as one of the nation's most promising scholars and writers. He had entered the University of Pennsylvania at the age of ten, and, ready for graduation at thirteen, was denied a degree because of his age. He then entered the College of New Jersey (Princeton), where he concentrated on the study of the classics and French literature and received his degree in 1801. Three years later the brilliant eighteen-year-old was appointed secretary to the American minister to France. He seized that occasion and his subsequent appointment as secretary of legation in London under Monroe to further his literary studies. Although admitted to the bar in 1809, he was more deeply committed to a literary career, collaborating with Joseph Dennie in his management of *The Port Folio* and, upon Dennie's death in 1812, succeeding to the editorship.

In delivering his expedition into the hands of this accomplished man of letters, Clark, the literate but unlettered man of action, sought to elevate the records he and Lewis had kept to a level of expressiveness that would make their expedition widely and lastingly known. Until documented in a variety of ways by the expedition, the western vastness was unknown to the Americans who were nibbling at its edges, but those documents nevertheless required translation in turn if they were to speak to more persons than the relatively few scientists, politicians, and adventurers who searched such data for particular ends.

As his title indicated, Biddle concentrated on creating from a

number of sources a single account that would stand as *the* history
of the expedition. He blended the separate journals kept by the
captains, other and briefer journals kept by two sergeants, Gass and
Ordway, and the oral glosses and additions he received in person
from Private Shannon, who was the expedition member sent by
Clark to assist in the writing. The result was an unflagging narrative
told in a polished manner that was at some distance from the blunt
notation and backwoods orthography of Clark and the more rum-
inative observations of Lewis, yet remarkably consistent in the tone
of voice Biddle created from the two in order to narrate the events
selected from the different journals. Reuben Gold Thwaites, who
edited and indexed the original journals and all the scientific data
and atlases for the 1904 edition, said that Biddle condensed nearly
1,500,000 words of manuscript into 370,000 printed words. "So
skillfully is the work done," Thwaites added, "that probably few
have realized that they had not before them the veritable journals
of the explorers themselves, written upon the spot."[6] In 1953, Bernard De Voto located the Biddle *History* among histories of the west:

> It was the first report on the West, on the United States over the
> hill and beyond the sunset, on the province of the American future.
> There has never been another so excellent or so influential. So it
> was rather as a treasury of knowledge than as a great adventure
> story that the *History* became a national and international favorite,
> reprinted, translated, pirated, and counterfeited.

When De Voto goes on to say that "the increase of our cultural
heritage, the beginning of knowledge of the American West, must
be accounted the most important result of the Lewis and Clark
expedition,"[7] that expedition as a series of events and a miscellany
of data has disappeared into the *History* which represented it. Clark
recorded his days, Lewis recorded his, and others, too, supplied
memories, written and oral, but the Lewis and Clark expedition was
not these but the history formed from them by a Philadelphia lawyer,
editor, and enthusiast of French literature.

Even the greatest adventures if they extend over many months contain a portion of uneventful days. Here is one such as entered in Clark's journal, "June the 15th Satturday 1805":

> a fair morning and worm, we set out at the usial time and proceeded on with great dificuelty as the river is more rapid we can hear the falls this morning very distinctly. our Indian woman sick & low spirited I gave her the bark & apply it exteranely to her region which revived her much. the current excessively rapid and dificuelt to assend great numbers of dangerous places, and the fatigue which we have to encounter is increatiable the men in the water from morning untill night hauling the cord & boats walkin on sharp rocks and round sliperery stone which alternately cut their feet & throw them down, notwith standing all this dificuelty they go with great chearfulness, added to those dificuelties the rattle snakes [are] inumerable & require great caution to prevent being bitten.[8]

The same day in Biddle's *History:* "Saturday 15—

> The morning being warm and fair we set out at the usual hour, but proceeded with great difficulty in consequence of the incessant rap idity of the current. The channel is constantly obstructed by rocks and dangerous rapids. During the whole progress the men are in the water hauling the canoes, and walking on sharp rocks and round stones which cut their feet or cause them to fall. The rattlesnakes are so numerous that the men are constantly on their guard against being bitten by them; yet they bear the fatigues with the most undiminished cheerfulness.[9]

It is difficult not to prefer Clark's "sliperery" or even a primmer "slippery" to Biddle's "round" stones, and his "throw them down" to "cause them to fall." There seems in Clark a greater appropriateness of diction to experience, and the sense of immediacy that Biddle reduces by altering the diction is further diminished by his syntax, which reorganizes and coheres details that Clark at times presents in detachment from one another and at times heaps together in run-on sentences. Moreover, a certain tactile feeling that Clark manages to communicate both in the details that are sometimes omitted by Biddle and in his very spelling is missing from the *History*.

But without Clark's journal before us, we read Biddle's *History* as a fluent, well-paced, yet descriptive account that develops its own aura of reality. Although the immediate world it creates is obviously literary, it is also consistently engaging as, indeed, the conventions of writing that it follows are designed to make it, whereas the attraction of authenticity exerted by Clark's journal gives way to weariness as one scrambles from phrase to phrase.

The greatest discrepancy between Biddle's and Clark's accounts occurs in the description of the Mandan buffalo dance, a ceremony that led Biddle to retreat into a purely literary language so at odds with its subject that its first effect is comic. Here writ large is an example of Biddle's insistent assimilation of the events of the expedition, however new or strange they may be for readers, to the conventions of literature. Under the date "5th of January Satturday 1805," Clark wrote:

> a Buffalow Dance (or Medeson) for 3 nights passed in the 1st Village, a curious Custom the old men arrange themselves in a circle & after Smoke[ing] a pipe which is handed them by a young man, Dress[ed] up for the purpose, the young men who have their wives back of the Circle go [each] to one of the old men with a whining tone and request the old man to take his wife (who presents [herself] necked except a robe) and—(or Sleep with her) the Girl then takes the Old Man (who verry often can scarcely walk) and leades him to a convenient place for the business, after which they return to the lodge; if the old man (or a white man) returns to the lodge without gratifying the Man & his wife, he offers her again and again; it is often the Case that after the 2d time without Kissing the Husband throws a new robe over the old man &c. and begs him not to dispise him & his wife (We sent a man to this Medisan Dance last night, they gave him 4 Girls) all this to cause the buffalow to Come near So that they may Kill them.

Biddle, who possessed supplementary information from his conversations with Shannon, translated Clark into his flowing English through the sentence, "the young men bring with them a platter of provisions, a pipe of tobacco, and their wives, whose dress on the occasion is only a robe or mantle loosely thrown round the body." But his next sentence is, *"Mox senex vir simulacrum parvae puellae ostensit,"* and he continues in Latin to the end of the entry in observance of the tradition that dictates that knowledge of value to science but potential damage to the unlearned be communicated in the code of the learned. Nevertheless, the distance between the buffalo dance and the Latin in which it is preserved may serve as a metaphor of the distance between a culture of immanence and the writing that in effect buries it even as it represents it. The language of the dance demands the body of the dancer; the language of the description is so removed from corporeal presence that it does not even need to be one that has speakers. The Latin entombs the Mandans.

Throughout their expedition the explorers counted upon the Indians' willingness to extend hospitality, give geographical information, and supply food either in trade or as gifts. The captains had no maps to follow, of course, and insofar as the land was known to their successive Indian informants it was known in tracts, each tribe familiar with its own range but none with the entire region the expedition was to traverse. The expedition, therefore, was both a journey into the unknown and a progress from one known to another, a passage through a chain of nations each of which had dealings beyond its borders so that, for example, Pacific Coast artifacts were encountered well east of the Rockies. Amicable relations prevailed almost throughout; violence flared rarely. No member of the expedition was killed, and although one Indian detected stealing horses was shot and killed by the soldiers this incident did not occur until the twenty-sixth of the twenty-eight months of the journey.

Indeed, the greatest danger the Indians could pose for Lewis and Clark arose from their absence rather than their presence. Without them the party could not have survived the Great Plains winter or have found the routes that permitted them to proceed without the losses of life and time that could have forced an end to their venture. Their moments of greatest anxiety were occasioned by failure to make contact with the people on whose homeland they were traveling.

The most pressing of such moments provides the most suspenseful part in both the journals and the *History*. When the party reached the headwaters of the Missouri in July 1805, they left their canoes and entered into the mountains in search of the sources of the Columbia River. Before they had entered upon the expedition they had had reason to hope that the distance between the headwaters of the east-flowing Missouri and the west-flowing Columbia was negligible, perhaps the matter of a few days' trek. But as they advanced westward and accumulated scraps of information, it became ominously probable that the distance was much greater, and that they would wander in the mountains to the point of starvation unless they encountered the natives of the region. They could neither discover the direction to take to the Columbia without Indian guidance nor make their way to it without Indian willingness to trade them horses. As they toiled on after leaving the Missouri, they desperately needed to make contact with the native tribes. But despite signs that the Indians were aware of their presence in the mountains, they could sight none. What was later to be a cliché in Western adventure fiction, the white man's seeing Indians and taking care to remain unseen by them, was reversed as they strained to see the Indians who they knew were seeing them in order to enter into dealings with them.

The strain was increased by the fact that Sacajawea now began to recognize the terrain. Born in a Snake (Shoshone) village (in the future state of Idaho) in 1800, she, at the age of thirteen, had been captured by a war party of Minnetaree (Hidastas) in the area of the Three Forks of the Missouri where now, in July 1805, the expedition

was casting about for direction. Taken to a Minnetaree village at
the mouth of the Knife River, the girl was sold to the hunter Toussaint Charbonneau, who married her as well as another young Indian
woman captured with her. At Fort Mandan, Charbonneau was engaged as an interpreter by Lewis and Clark with the understanding
that Sacajawea would accompany the party (she carried an infant
born February 1805 with her), and their frustration at failing to
make contact with the Snakes was aggravated by the expectation of
the favorable reception Sacajawea's presence would gain them. If
only the unseen Indians watching them would come forward!

On July 27, 1805, Lewis wrote:

> we begin to feel considerable anxiety with rispect to the Snake
> Indians. if we do not find them or some other nation who have
> horses I fear the successful issue of our voyage will be very doubtfull
> or at all events much more difficult in it's accomplishment. we are
> now several hundred miles within the bosom of this wild and moun-
> tanous country, where game may rationally be expected shortly to
> become scarce and subsistence precarious without any information
> with rispect to the country nor knowing how far these mountains
> continue, or wher to direct our course to pass them to advantage
> or intersept a navigable branch of the Columbia, or even were we
> on such an one the probability is that we should not find any timber
> within these mountains large enough for canoes if we judge from
> the portion of them through which we have passed. however I still
> hope for the best and intend taking a tramp myself in a few days
> to find these yellow gentlemen if possible. my two principal con-
> solations are that from our present position it is impossible that the
> S. W. fork can head with the waters of any other river but the
> Columbia, and that if any Indians can subsist in the form of a nation
> in these mountains with the means they have of acquiring food we
> can also subsist.

Although Lewis was aware of the likelihood that others would
read his journal, his entries are addressed primarily to himself (as
are Clark's to himself). The recording of his situation is inseparable

from his reflecting upon it; he uses his journal, that is, not just as an aid to memory in the future but as a means of thinking about the present. The entry just cited takes stock of what is described, points to the only action that can be taken, and concludes with words of self-comforting that arise not from the situation but from the act of having assessed it in writing.

Biddle's version follows responsibly, but his text is addressed to a reader so that his speaker is made to explain how things stand to a third party rather than to himself:

> We are now very anxious to see the Snake Indians. After advancing for several hundred miles into this wild and mountainous country, we may soon expect that the game will abandon us. With no information on the route we may be unable to find a passage across the mountains when we reach the head of the river, at least such a one as will lead us to the Columbia, and even were we so fortunate as to find a branch of that river, then timber which we have hitherto seen in these mountains does not promise us any fit to make canoes, so that our chief dependence is on meeting some tribes from whom we may procure horses. Our consolation is, that the southwest branch can scarcely head with any other river than the Columbia, and that if any nation of Indians can live in the mountains we are able to endure as much as they, and have even better means of subsistence.

The differences in content between this and Lewis's original are slight. But the effect is different because Biddle rearranges the sentence elements that Lewis recorded in the order in which they entered his mind into complex sentences that have already determined what is cause and what effect, what is primary and what contingent. Experience is thus conveyed to the reader as already mediated by thought—Biddle's more literary diction furthering this effect—rather than as presenting itself to the mind. The experience of the narrator(s) is subordinated to the literary expectations of the reader, and wherever Indian life enters it is subordinated to the culture of the literate society that reads about it rather than encountered as the expedition encountered it. Lewis and Clark, who served an imperial politics and told each tribe they met that the Great White Father was now the man in Washington, did not in their daily dealings subordinate Indian culture to theirs. It was Biddle's *History* that added cultural to political imperialism.

Or perhaps it is more accurate to say that Indians were subjugated to the new Americans in proportion to the refinement of the language employed not only in describing but in communicating with them. Notice, for example, the language of the long-desired first encounter with the Snakes. Desperate to make contact, a party led by Lewis had for some days been following Indian tracks when, on August 13, 1805, they suddenly came upon three women. Because of the ravined terrain, neither Lewis's group nor the women saw one another until they were thirty paces apart. One woman fled, but an elderly woman and a girl of about twelve remained, "holding down their heads," says Lewis, "as if reconciled to die." (Biddle cannot resist adding, "The same habit of holding down the head and inviting the enemy to strike when all chance of escape is gone, is preserved in Egypt to this day.") Having put down his gun, Lewis reports, "I took the elderly woman by the hand and raised her up repeated the word *tab-ba-bone* and strip[ped] up my shirt sleve to s[h]ew her my skin; to prove to her the truth of the ascertion that I was a white man for my face and ha[n]ds which have been constantly exposed to the sun were quite as dark as their own." After giving the women presents of beads, moccasin awls, pewter looking glasses, and paint, Lewis proceeded to the next step in nurturing so fragile yet crucial a relationship. He asked Drewyer (Drouillet), his interpreter, "to request the old woman to recall the young woman who had run off to some distance by this time fearing she might allarm the camp before we approached and might so exasperate the natives that they would perhaps attack us without enquiring who we were." This was accomplished, and "I bestoed an equ[i]volent

portion of trinket on her with the other. I now painted their tawny
cheeks with some vermillion which with this nation is emblematic
of peace." The women then led the party to their encampment, and
the relations were commenced that resulted in the expedition's successful negotiation of the Bitterroot Mountains to the Columbia's
headwaters.

The one Indian word Lewis did use was not effective until
supported by the display of his body. The relationship initiated by
the giving of gifts was confirmed when Lewis's fingers passed back
and forth over the women's cheeks as he painted them. And even
when he relied upon his interpreter, he was at but one remove from
such bodily statement. He says:

> The means I had of communicating with these people was by
> way of Drewyer who understood perfectly the common language
> of jesticulation or signs which seems to be universally understood
> by all the Nations we have yet seen. it is true that this language is
> imperfect and liable to error but is much less so than would be
> expected. the strong parts of the ideas are seldom mistaken.

As A. L. Kroeber observes, the Plains Indian sign language is
almost totally pantomimic: "Speech consists overwhelmingly of elements wholly without transparent or inherent resemblance of symbol
to signification, but the sign language elements overwhelmingly do
show such connection between gesture and meaning."[10] Since the
signs are not grounded in words, those who use them recognize the
limits of what they can express and thus of the understanding they
can achieve. While this restricts their communication to elementary
things, it also promotes an equality between them. Each recognizes
that he has left the stronghold of his native tongue to meet on
neutral ground where neither can impose his thoughts upon the
other or sway him emotionally. Only when the captains with the
aid of interpreters were able to use speech could they communicate
the political message of American empire. Words destabilized

the equality that was a condition of sign language and enabled them to assert the authority of their nation over that of their hearers.

On May 11, 1806, during the early stage of the return journey east, the expedition visited the Choppunish (Nez Percés) in the southeastern part of the present state of Washington. They found among them a Snake boy who had been captured on one of the Choppunish's eastward raids into the mountains, even as Sacajawea had earlier been captured by the Minnetarees on one of their westward raids. These two formed the central links in the verbal chain that permitted the captains to tell the Choppunish of the new American hegemony. The captains spoke in English to one of their men who spoke in French to Charbonneau who spoke in Minnetaree to Sacajawea who spoke in Snake to the Snake boy who spoke in Choppunish to his captors. Clark wrote that "the interpretation being tegious it occupied the greater part of the day, before we had communicated to them what we wished." And what they wished to communicate was "the view of our government with respect to the inhabitants of this Western part of the Continent, their intentions of establishing tradeing houses for their relief, their wish to restore peace and harmony among the nativs, the strength welth and powers of our nation &c." The message was accompanied by the drawing of an illustrative map upon a mat with a piece of coal, and the good will of the United States was demonstrated by Clark, who dispensed the contents of his medicine chest for the relief of scrofula, ulcers, rheumatism, and sore eyes. Even with interpreters available, words were not far from physical signs.

Still, the message of imperialism was sent and received only when principal reliance could be placed upon words, and, ominously, the crucial agents in this transmission, Sacajawea and the Snake boy, had acquired their second languages at the cost of their freedom. Captivity was the precondition for intertribal linguistic exchange within oral cultures. This cause and effect relationship, however, was reversed within the written culture of Americans. In the pages of the great majority of those who wrote about Indians—from Jefferson well on into the nineteenth century, including, preeminently, James Fenimore Cooper—language did the capturing, binding Indian society to a future of certain extinction. Treating living Indians as sources for a literary construction of a vanished way of life rather than as members of a vital continuing culture, such writers used words to replace rather than to represent Indian reality.

Lewis and Clark knew otherwise. As their party required Indian assistance to meet its need for food, transportation, guidance, social interchange, and sexual gratification, they developed a respect for the integrity and coherence of societies that had mastered such needs in keeping with the particular conditions of their various environments, most of them severely trying. They dealt with the Indians as equals. With its bodily medium, close resemblance between symbol and signification, and dependence upon a physically responsive receiver, sign language may be taken as the instrument of equality of exchange between two cultures. When sign language gave way to interpreted speech, even as the recorded facts and unmediated impressions of the travelers gave way to the written history of the expedition, so cultural equality gave way to dominance and the process of literary annihilation.

Literary annihilation, in which the representation offers itself as the only aspect of the represented that is still extant, is not, of course, physical extermination. Indeed, writers such as Jefferson and Dwight, or Cooper after them, sincerely regarded their writings as efforts at preservation. But they memorialized rather than perpetuated, and by writing Indian history as obituary they unconsciously collaborated with those bent on physical extermination. What Cooper regarded as distinctive and valuable in Indian culture, for example, he treated as if on the far side of a temporal abyss. It existed in a time that he represented as sealed off from the present; the resulting dramatic discontinuity between the time about which he wrote and the time in which he wrote the major Indian novels enabled the reader to enjoy a museumlike visit to Indian culture without the need to connect it to his present.[11] The process of literary annihilation would be checked only when Indian writers began representing their own culture. As whites had utilized sign language to commence their dialogue with Indians, so Indians, finally, would come to utilize the conventions of written English to restore dialogue to what for a century after Biddle's *History* had been in reality a monologue with the Indian's voice supplied by the ventriloquizing culture of the white.

CHAPTER NINE

WILD USAGES

The Sensitive Frontiersman: Filson and Cooper—The Savage Frontiersman:
Brown and Bird—Wildness and Democracy: Ethan Allen—The Wild Man in
the Margin: Melville and Emerson

*T*HE message that flowed from the new Americans to the
Indians bound the receivers to the senders' goods, government, and language. To be sure, an important strand
of European thought sought to reverse this direction,
insisting that the Indian in the purity of his separation from the
artifices of civilization and his immersion in a life led in response
to the rhythms of nature could be seen as a guide to the rejuvenation
of an exhausted European culture. Although the noble savage who
filled this role was a creation of social philosophers, once he existed
on the page those who responded to his symbolic significance also
located him in the life. William Bartram, for example, saw such
models of social conduct when he visited the Creeks, and Chateaubriand, informed by Bartram's book before he visited the United
States, accordingly encountered noble savages when he made his
visit. From Bartram in the 1770s to James Fenimore Cooper in the
1840s, there were American writers who sought to open their culture
to the redeeming influence of American nature and the people who
inhabited it and to suggest the loss suffered by a society that overrode
Indian reality. But even these champions of untamed nature tamed
it in the act of praising it.

When Meriwether Lewis sought to express the effect upon him of natural scenery never before viewed by lettered man, he consulted his aesthetic training. Viewing the lower of the Great Falls of the Missouri and conscious of being the first person ever to record a description of it, he told his journal that he longed for the pen of the poet James Thomson or the pencil of the painter Salvator Rosa. And when, after this overwhelming sight, the next day he came upon the equally overwhelming upper falls, he searched for a way to distinguish the effect of the one from that of the other while doing justice to both and found it in the neoclassical vocabulary of natural description. Before the upper falls on June 14, 1805, he wrote, "I now thought that if a skillful painter had been asked to make a beautiful cascade that he would most probably have p[r]esented the precise immage of this one; nor could I for some time determine on which of those two great cataracts to bestoe the palm, on this or that which I had discovered yesterday; at length I determined between these two great rivals for glory that this was *pleasingly beautifull,* while the other was *sublimely grand.*"[1]

Literary culture similarly came to the aid of writers who sought ways to characterize the unprecedented and, they thought, definitively American type, the frontiersman, who stood halfway between the European and the Indian, white by birth and Christian by baptism but Indian in habits and pantheistic in perception. Unique as was this figure in the flesh, he found his way onto the page in terms that had been made popular by the sentimentalizing style of Laurence Sterne. The literary prototype of this isolate, unlettered hunter whose instructors were Indians and whose curriculum was woodcraft yet whose ultimate allegiance was to the society that encroached upon the wilderness he loved, a figure who achieved his apotheosis in Cooper's Natty Bumppo, was the Daniel Boone of "The adventures of Colonel Daniel Boon," which the land speculator John Filson appended to his *Kentucke* (1784) as a further means of extolling the glories of a region in which he had acquired land warrants and so wished to promote. Although narrated in the first person as if by Boone, the account is manifestly the work of Filson, who had spoken with Boone while preparing his book.

As doughty a scout, hunter, Indian fighter, and adopted Indian as Boone was, these characteristics are overshadowed in the narrative by the sensibility that reports them and in so doing responds feelingly to its natural surroundings. For example, after recounting how in the six months since he left his family in Virginia he had scouted unmapped Kentucky, been captured by Indians, escaped, and then faced a continued life in the wilds accompanied only by his brother, Filson's Boone says:

> Thus situated many hundred miles from our families in the howling wilderness, I believe few would have equally enjoyed the happiness we experienced: I often observed to my brother, you see how little nature requires to be satisfied. Felicity, the companion of content, is rather found in our own breasts than in the enjoyment of external things.[2]

Such refinement faces its severest test when, his brother having returned home, Boone in May 1770 begins his second year in Kentucky absolutely alone, without even horse or dog and with no provisions whatsoever, no bread, salt, or sugar. He admits that in the first few days of his solitude he suffered "dreadful apprehensions." But the effect of his surroundings soon overcome his misgivings, because "No populous city, with all the varieties of commerce and stately structures, could afford so much pleasure to my mind, as the beauties of nature I found here" (*Kentucke,* p. 56).

To follow Filson's Boone further is to encounter additional examples of the discrepancy between the actions of the rough and ready hunter and the language of sentimental reflection in which he presents himself. And the discrepancy finally compels a separation within the character of Boone himself. As the conventional language increasingly controls the nature of the experience, Boone both enjoys his solitude yet asks that we feel for his loneliness, revels in his explorations yet asks that we see them as a sacrifice of self for the greater good, thrills to the sublimity of unspoiled nature yet asks that we recognize him as the agent of a god bent on reducing that nature to tillage. At the close Boone is made to say:

> Two darling sons, and a brother, have I lost by savage hands, which have also taken from me forty valuable horses, and abundance of cattle. Many dark and sleepless nights have I been a companion for owls, separated from the chearful society of men, scorched by the Summer's sun, and pinched by the Winter's cold, an instrument ordained to settle the wilderness. But now the scene is changed: Peace crowns the sylvan shade. (*Kentucke,* pp. 80–81)

The language of the Bible, of pastoral, and of sentimentalism merge in these sentences to effect Boone's translation into literary conventionalism, understandable in terms of the shreds of meaning that cling to well-gnawed phrases such as "companion of owls," "instrument ordained," and "sylvan shade," rather than in any terms prompted by his having shared the stage with the Shawnees in a decade-long drama of mutual antagonism, admiration, killing, adoption, and adaptation.

Cooper's Natty Bumppo inherited Boone's separated self, but Cooper's literary intelligence converted this condition from contradiction to complexity, and, as a result, elevated Natty to the level of myth. Natty speaks for the law of nature that had reigned before the white man arrived to replace it with the legal codes that, in effect, first brought lawlessness to the new world. In the previous epoch the entire creation was instinct with natural law. Now, however, Natty must speak for it and since in this very verbalizing he removes it from its site in the unconscious mind, he, in effect, enacts its demise. Parallel to the self-cancellation implicit in this articulation of a law that once articulated ceases to be law is the more obvious self-cancellation that occurs when Natty's successive flights from white society into nature result in his blazing the trail that society follows.

Filson emphasized Boone's sensibility in order to demonstrate that migration to Kentucky would not coarsen the character but, on the contrary, refine it. Although Cooper was alarmed by the effect the wasteful ways of the settlers had upon the wild, his alarm proceeded from a belief in the ameliorating influence of nature that he shared with Filson.

Over the same period (1790s to 1840s) other writers advanced an opposing view, that the wilderness drew forth the violence that people repressed in society. With his astute eye for psychological process, Charles Brockden Brown in *Edgar Huntly* (1799) created the earliest as well as the best of the novels that dramatized this connection between wild nature and the release of the violent self, and did so, moreover, in apparent endorsement of the ultimately beneficial effects of white savagery when practiced against red savages.

At the start of the novel, Edgar, walking to his home on the edge of the forest during the night, spies a man digging under an elm. He pauses unseen to muse upon the sight, asking, "Was his purpose to explore or to hide? Was it proper to watch him at a distance, unobserved, and in silence, or to rush upon him and extort from him by violence or menaces, an explanation of the scene?"[3] The conflict between secrecy and revelation that is sounded at the outset, wherein disclosure of the hidden is linked to violence, becomes a dominant theme in the novel as the attempt to reach the hidden self is symbolized in scenes involving the penetration of locked chests in bedrooms and hidden caves in the forest as well as digging in the earth.

Having been attracted by Clithero, the man he discovered digging, Edgar begins to shadow him, and as he becomes better acquainted with him, so we, the readers, become aware that although Edgar does not initially recognize it, his mirroring of Clithero's movements proceeds from similarities they share; his obsessive pursuit of the other man is also a hounding of himself. As his focus on his double narrows to monomania, so the signs of identification between the two increase until Edgar, like Clithero, also becomes a sleepwalker, revealing his repressed self in actions over which he has no conscious control. In a crucial sequence of events, the sleepwalking Edgar rises from his bed and wanders through the forest to a pitlike cave where he once again lies down. Awakening there he thinks at first that he has been mistaken for dead and entombed, then, dimly gathering his bearings, he struggles to emerge from the cave. It is night once again, and he finds his way blocked by a panther that he kills and, to appease his raging appetite, proceeds to eat raw. Again he falls into sleep, to be awakened by a desperate thirst. Driven by it he goes in search of water only to encounter a band of raiding Indians whom he ambushes, and, after killing four of them, he again falls asleep. When he regains consciousness he finds his head pillowed on the breast of one of the slain Indians and his hair matted with the blood that oozed from his victim. Thus bloodied he goes on to kill a fifth Indian, and after some further adventures in which he mistakes friends for Indians even as they mistake him for an Indian—his preferred weapon throughout is the tomahawk—he returns to the settlements. Horrific as are the details, in the reading they escape mere sensationalism because of their subordination to the psychological drama they enact.

Thinking about what he had done (or undergone) in the forest, Edgar remarks, "I had emerged from abhorred darkness, only to endure the extremities of famine and encounter the fangs of a wild beast. From these I was delivered only to be thrown into the midst of savages, to wage an endless and hopeless war with adepts in killing; with appetites that longed to feast upon my bowels and to quaff my heart's-blood" (*Edgar Huntly,* pp. 223–24). Although he thus sees himself as having been passive through all the violence—he "was delivered" from the panther and "was rescued" from the Indians against whom he was "hopeless"—the reader has seen that he not only killed both panther and Indians but had eaten the flesh of the former and bathed his head in the blood of the latter. He was the "adept in killing" and his was the appetite that did not just long for but feasted on its enemy. But he sees himself as the moved rather than the mover because the rationalizing self that does the reflecting was indeed passive before the outburst of the unconscious self that killed.

Indian-white relations are not the theme of *Edgar Huntly,* the Indians functioning rather as figures in a psychological drama. But in making the Indians nighttime agents of violence and associating them with the scenario of the unconscious—the Indian woman who inspired the raiding party is named Queen Mab—Brown captures the state of mind that pushed society into violence against Indians as those who dealt explicitly with Indian-white relations did not. Edgar embodies in his person the link between savage behavior and civilized rationale that was accepted by many in his society who viewed themselves as passive instruments. They believed the savagery they evinced was not theirs but the Indians', and they depersonalized their violence by regarding it as part of a delivery from danger in which they were but the agents of a cosmic scheme—the divine plan for the continent or the political destiny of the American people.

In *Nick of the Woods* (1837), Robert Montgomery Bird, a Philadelphia-based author as Brown had been before him, provided the most fascinating, if also violently sensational, of the novels that dramatized a white savagery that went beyond any Indian behavior and justified it in terms of the advancement of civilization. The plot in good part is a dark parody of Cooper's *Last of the Mohicans* (1826), and its central character, Nathan Slaughter, is a grim caricature of Natty Bumppo, resembling him in outward manner while secretly being an Indian hater of psychopathic dimensions. Like Edgar's author, Nathan's provides him with an excuse for his animosity—his family was massacred by Indians before the action of the novel proper commenced—but like Edgar's also, Nathan's savagery exceeds any such motive. He murders Indians from racial hate, simply because they are Indians, and he both scalps them and hacks his mark upon their breasts. Like Brown, Bird suggests that his character is out of his mind when in his murderous frenzies, yet Bird does not, for all that, disavow the killing. In order to conquer the savage one had to outdo him in savagery, and this was so far from being regarded as illogical that it was represented as psychologically therapeutic as well as socially beneficial, because the wild man within was purged even as the wild man without was exterminated. For Brown, the social benefit followed from the psychological release; for Bird, the social benefit licensed the psychological release. In both cases, after madness and killing, reason and civilization resumed their sway, all the better for the cathartics.

Along the line from Filson to Cooper the theme was one that lauded the influence of American nature upon American character even as it projected the inevitable end of wilderness and the replacement of natural with civil law. Wild nature's literary function was to illustrate the aesthetic of the sublime, the beautiful, and the picturesque. No specific political function grew from the effect of American nature upon those who lived in its midst, although, to be sure, in a general way more sensitive individuals made better citizens.

Along the line from Brown to Bird the theme was one of the way American nature called forth the wildness in the American character. Wild nature's literary function was to allegorize the drama of the psyche. No specific political function grew from this evocation of wildness although, more generally, wild white men cleared the way for settlement. But as Timothy Dwight expressed it, such men were not the founders of society "but seem to be of no other use than to remove the difficulties which might discourage the attempts of better and more quiet men."[4]

~~~~~~~~~~~~~~~

Understandably, in a young republic uncertain of the stability of its institutions and fearful of either a collapse into anarchy or a preventive imposition of oligarchical government, any wild streak in the body politic was seen as a threat. But by the close of the 1820s, as Andrew Jackson's election to the presidency indicated, the fear of anarchy had largely dissipated, hastened in good part by a widespread distaste for the perceived authoritarianism of Federalist measures during the John Quincy Adams administration. And with such fear dissipated, the notion that American democracy relied upon a degree of wildness for its preservation gained popular acceptance. Rather than being seen as the crude precursors of those who actually established civil society, the bold and savage frontiersmen came to be regarded as the founders and guardians of American society.

In the days immediately following the Revolution, however, only one work, *A Narrative of Colonel Ethan Allen's Captivity* (1798), embodied that idea, and in so doing foreshadowed what was in the succeeding period to be developed as typically American both in popular literature and in the writings of Emerson, Thoreau, Whitman, and Melville. The author of that narrative was indeed Ethan Allen himself rather than any Filson-like promoter, and an unabashedly self-vaunting Ethan Allen at that. His self-presentation was a vigorous assertion of the useful political consequences of an Indian-like fierceness, if not savagery.

Born in Connecticut in 1738, Ethan Allen at around the age of thirty took up residence in Vermont, where he initially raised the celebrated Green Mountain Boys in order to defend New Hampshire's claims to Vermont against those of New York. He pursued his end with such vehemence that Governor Tryon of New York offered a reward for his capture, but the outbreak of the American Revolution put this dispute aside and prepared another captivity for Allen.

After his celebrated victory at Ticonderoga in May 1775, Allen led an attempt on Montreal that resulted in his capture in September of that year. He was transported to England, and, while a prisoner there, was often exhibited to visitors eager to see the conquered conqueror of Ticonderoga. Viewing celebrated prisoners was not an unusual diversion for gentle as well as common folk, but Allen amplified it into high spectacle by building on his reputation as a frontier warrior to act out the character of the wild man from the American woods. He thrilled female visitors with his feats of strength then titillated them with the gallant words that issued from his burly, uncouth person, and he alternately incensed and amused the males with his outrageously disrespectful comments on royalty and its supporters, pointedly contrasting his shaggy person with their foppish carriage. Returned to America and held a prisoner in British-occupied New York, Allen was finally exchanged in May 1778 and within a year wrote and published his *Narrative,* thereby capitalizing on the notoriety he had gained both as the hero of Ticonderoga and the untameable woodsman who had bearded the British lion even when kept chained in that lion's den.

To his contemporary Timothy Dwight, Allen in his bluster appeared to be all too typical of the class of Americans he deplored: "Licentious in his disposition, he was impatient at the restraints either of government or religion, and not always submissive to those of common decency" (*Travels in New England and New York,* 2:283). His towering self-confidence, Dwight said, misled those still less informed into trusting in him. The message Allen's self-confidence conveyed to others, however, was not that they should trust him so much as that they should trust themselves and not submit to restraints that insulted their natural feelings.

As in all captivity narratives, the framing story in Allen's is that of the desire for and eventual achievement of freedom. The energy of his account, however, comes not from this but from the furious and sometimes comic intensity with which he conducted another struggle within this frame, a struggle to wrest from his captors the recognition that he was a gentleman. Superficially, his claim to this title and the British rejection of it were a matter of the interpretation of military protocol. Since Allen did not hold a commission in the

American army but was an elected officer in the militia, it was questionable whether he merited treatment as an officer and therefore a gentleman. Some charged with overseeing him treated him as a common rebel who was lucky to be alive even under the harshest prison conditions since he deserved hanging.[5] But Allen's campaign to be treated as a gentleman quickly exceeded debates about the rules of war because he challenged the idea of a social hierarchy inherent in the traditional concept of the gentleman and forced his captors to confront his person and not his rank or social standing as the chief evidence of his worth. Moreover, he did not attempt to clothe that person in the costume or manners conventionally associated with a gentleman but insisted on basing his claims for respect on the self-evident manhood of his independent bearing, which he did not hesitate to demonstrate theatrically so that none would mistake him.

Allen's *Narrative* suggests a parallel between the condition of the colonies under British rule and his condition as a prisoner so that his personal freedom is conflated with national independence. But the larger symbolic force of his account comes from his identification of his wild behavior with the cause of democracy and his suggestion that the suppression of the many in a monarchy relies upon a prior reduction of a natural instinct for liberty that derives from man's original wild condition. The more severely Allen is confined the fiercer becomes his behavior as he counters every increase in restraint with an increased release of unchecked feelings. On board a hellish prison ship he says, "I was obliged to throw out plenty of extravagant language, which answered certain purposes (at that time) better than to grace history" (*Narrative*, p. 28). And so antic was his behavior under confinement in New York that "the enemy gave out that I was crazy, and wholly unmanned, but my vitals held sound (nor was I delirious any more than I have been from my youth up, but my circumstances at certain times, rendered it political to act in some measure the madman)" (*Narrative*, pp. 77–78). For Allen, psychological and political revolution are linked.

Alexander Graydon, who encountered Allen when both were prisoners of war in New York, registered the extraordinary force of his presence. While Allen was acting the madman, Graydon was reinforcing the claims to gentility he derived from his officer's commission with an exhibition of polished manners that gained him treatment as a gentleman from the British officers and invitations to the dinner tables of the city's leading Tory families. He was such a stickler for form that he even insisted upon the need to be well dressed when conducting a revolution: "In civil contests it is highly requisite for the party in opposition to government, to counteract the advantage of recognized authority, by an appearance that may raise them above contempt."[6] And if this were not sufficient ground for him to dislike Allen, he had in addition a broad aversion to the graceless ways of New England Yankees, as revealed especially by their dress, saying, for example, that General Israel Putnam of Connecticut "riding with a hanger belted across his brawny shoulders over a waistcoat without sleeves (his summer costume) was deemed much fitter to head a band of sickle-men or ditchers, than musketeers" (*Memoirs,* pp. 156–57). Predictably, when the polished Graydon saw his fellow prisoner Allen, he noted "the insubordinate lawless frontier spirit in his composition." But the magnetism of Allen's elemental energy broke through the stuffiness of Graydon's intense propriety to force an admiration for the savagery blended into his composition and suggest that this was distinctively American. "I have seldom met a man," Graydon wrote, "possessing, in my opinion, a stronger mind, or whose mode of expression was more vehement and oratorical. His style was a singular compound of local barbarisms, scriptural phrases, and oriental wildness; and though unclassic and some times ungrammatical, it was highly animated and forcible" (*Memoirs,* p. 223). This characterization appears to have been drawn from the manner in which Allen represents himself in the *Narrative* as well as from direct observation. The figure who emerges on Graydon's page blends biblical with Indian primitivism and expresses himself with impressive effectiveness despite his scanty learning because of the sheer force with which his personal presence finds its outlet in oratory.

A half-century later, Herman Melville introduced Ethan Allen into his *Israel Potter* (1855), a novel centered on the theme of its protagonist's drift into anomie. An American seaman in the Revolution, Israel is captured and taken to England whence, as the result of one petty circumstance after another, he is unable to return to the United States even after the war. His loss of homeland leads to a loss of national identity—adrift in England he no longer knows what it is or feels like to be American—which, in turn, erases his personal identity. Ethan Allen, an American for whom English captivity heightened the sense of national identity, serves Melville as Israel's foil.

For his description, Melville drew upon details in Allen's *Narrative* but then organized and elaborated them in keeping with Graydon's impression of the singular mixture that went into Allen's style. The portrait of Allen is first drawn when Israel glimpses Allen the prisoner in England as Graydon had glimpsed Allen the prisoner in New York:

> The stranger was outlandishly arrayed in the sorry remains of a half-Indian, half-Canadian sort of a dress, consisting of a fawn-skin jacket—the fur outside and hanging in ragged tufts—a half-rotten bark-like belt of wampum; aged breeches of sagathy; bedarned worsted stockings to the knee; old moccasins riddled with holes, their metal tags yellow with salt-water rust; a faded red woolen bonnet, not unlike a Russian night-cap, or a portentous ensanguined full-moon, all soiled, and stuck about with bits of half-rotted straw. He seemed just broken from the dead leaves in David's outlawed Cave of Adullam. Unshaven, beard and hair matted, and profuse as a corn-field beaten down by hailstorms, his whole marred aspect was that of some wild beast; but of a royal sort, and unsubdued by the cage.[7]

With a fervid Old Testament attachment of self-righteousness to a higher cause and an unaffected fierceness of appearance that links him with the Indians of his native woods, Allen is Melville's essential American, the personification of the democratic spirit.

On another level of the culture, the popularity in Melville's day of the character of Davy Crockett (as represented in the various narratives of his life—one of them, that of 1834, "Written by Himself"—and the anecdotes retailed in the Crockett almanacs, the periodical press, and theatrical entertainments) illustrates the wide acceptance of the notion that the traits personified by Allen were those of the essential American democrat. In those representations, Crockett roamed restlessly through the canebreak, hunting varmints and battling Indians with a deadly sureness that arose from his kinship with them. Governed by the same instincts, he anticipated their every move and, as the tall tales that grew from the factual base of his skill as a bear hunter reveal, his killings were not acts of aggression so much as performances in a ritual of intimacy between him and the creatures with whom he identified. They talked to him in his language and he imitated them in his dress. In pictorial representations, Crockett's celebrated coonskin (or, in earlier versions, wildcat skin) cap enveloped him as if a whole animal had been joined to his head.

Both Crockett and his hagiographers stressed that he had been elected to Congress because the wildness he manifested was a guarantee of his being a fit representative of free men. His near illiteracy ("it will be a source of astonishment to many, who reflect that I am now a member of the American Congress,—the most enlightened body of men in the world,—that at so advanced an age, the age of fifteen, I did not know the first letter in the book"[8]) placed a premium upon his forcefulness as an orator and served as a further sign of his unshakeable untameability.

His dress, his living by the hunt, and his restless westering have led cultural historians to situate Crockett in the tradition of Filson's Boone and Cooper's Bumppo. But the similarity is all on the surface. Crockett does not share in the refinement of character the others derive from their life in nature but, on the contrary, insists upon retaining his savage streak even in cultured society. Most important, Crockett stands for the connection between such wildness and the welfare of the body politic, whereas Boone and Bumppo leave their wildness at the door when they step into the settlements. Ethan Allen is the closer kin.

~eeeeee(e℗℗ee))))eeee~

Emerson, Thoreau, and Whitman, as well as Melville, reacted against a submission to literary conventions that, they believed, so homogenized whatever was treated in accordance with them that America was not to be seen in American writings. The critique of literary culture that they mounted in their several ways contended that the revolutionary promise of the realization of individual power had been arrested by an attachment to forms extraneous to American life, and they asserted the primacy of flux over form and the physical or immanent over the intellectualized or mediated. In their search for ways to resolve the paradox of representing immanence—what Whitman meant when he said that he offered not poems but the origin of poems[9]—they invoked the figure of preliterary man, primitive or savage and frequently an Indian, as a standard of authenticity.

Sometimes the wild figure was at the center of the text, but his usual position was in the margin where he served to correct or ironize the text's tendency to drift into conventional representation by sheer dint of the fact that it was a literary text. Melville exemplifies this use in *Pierre* (1852), when the wild figure is invoked to devastate the literary efforts of the character, Pierre, and, by extension, of Melville the author who like Pierre in the novel is endeavoring to create a novel. Seated at his table in a barren, cold room, Pierre struggles at his writing even as Melville is at the same moment writing about Pierre writing:

> Pierre is young; heaven gave him the divinest, freshest form of man; put light into his eye, and fire into his blood; and brawn into

his arm, and a joyous, jubilant, overflowing, up-bubbling, universal life in him everywhere. Now look around in that most miserable room, and at that most miserable of all the pursuits of a man, and say if here be the place, and this be the trade, that God intended him for. A rickety chair, two hollow barrels, a plank, paper, pens, and infernally black ink, four leperously dingy white walls, no carpet, a cup of water, and a dry biscuit or two. Oh, I hear the leap of the Texan Camanche, as at this moment he goes crashing like a wild deer through the green underbrush; I hear his glorious whoop of savage and untameable health; and then I look in at Pierre. If physical, practical unreason make the savage, which is he? Civilization, Philosophy, Ideal Virtue! behold your victim.[10]

"The friendly and flowing savage, who is he?" Whitman asked, "Is he waiting for civilization, or past it and mastering it?" (*Song of Myself*, ll. 976–77). And Thoreau, perhaps the most self-conscious craftsman of the three, used the Indian to illustrate his conviction that the best-wrought writing erased the marks of its literariness: "The talent of composition is very dangerous,—the striking out the heart of life at a blow, as the Indian takes off a scalp."[11]

"It is almost the sole deduction from the merit of Plato," Emerson wrote of one of his most powerful influences, "that his writings have not,—what is, no doubt, incident to this regnancy of intellect in his work,—the vital authority which the screams of prophets and the sermons of unlettered Arabs and Jews possess. There is an interval; and to cohesion, contact is necessary."[12] The intellectual and the literary can but reach at the meaning contained in the nature that rages all about us. Its spirit resides in the unlettered utterances of those who experience the current that runs the circuit from themselves to elemental nature and back again.

Plato, Shakespeare, Napoleon—these are some of Emerson's "representative men." They exemplify power we all possess but have not realized in the degree they have. Man develops from within, Emerson asserts, and education is a matter of unfolding. "The aid we have from others," he continues, "is mechanical compared with the discoveries of nature in us" (*Essays and Lectures,* p. 617), and his representative men serve, finally, to lead us to those discoveries.

The Benjamin Franklin of the *Autobiography* is another kind of representative man, exemplifying the way one who shapes himself to his society will, in turn, shape society. As Benjamin Vaughan wrote in a letter Franklin included in the *Autobiography,* "all that has happened to you is also connected with the details of the manners and situation of *a rising* people."[13] Individuals, Franklin affirms, develop from without. Education is a matter of acquiring—habits as well as knowledge—and the aid we receive from others is crucial.

Representative men such as the Franklin of the *Autobiography* have power conferred upon them by their fellows who feel that they typify the common interest, whereas Emerson's representative men confer power on their fellows through leading them to self-discovery. Franklin's notion of representativeness is centripetal, pulling the individual into society to find his identity, Emerson's centrifugal, separating him from the mass of his fellows to find it. Franklin's self-made man makes himself in terms of a social world; indeed, he is "made" when that world recognizes his membership in it and extends him credit and confidence. Emerson's self-reliant man, on the other hand, can realize himself only when he frees himself from the net of social obligations:

> There are two confessionals, in one or the other of which we must be shriven. You may fulfil your round of duties by clearing yourself in the *direct,* or in the *reflex* way. Consider whether you have satisfied your relations to father, mother, cousin, neighbour, town, cat, and dog; whether any of them can upbraid you. But I may also neglect this reflex standard, and absolve me to myself. I have my own stern claims and perfect circle. It denies the name of duty to many offices that are called duties. But if I can discharge its debts, it enables me

to dispense with the popular code. If any one imagines that this law is lax, let him keep its commandments one day. (*Essays and Lectures,* p. 274)

In Franklin's world, the mass of men through the agency of representative government had come into the distinction denied them by the doctrine of hereditary rights. They had formed themselves into a collectivity and averaged their interests in choosing representatives. This transfer of power from immanence to representation had prevented mob rule, the exercise of power through the sheer weight of the corporeal mass, while at the same time assuring the rule of the people. More than a half-century later, Emerson was concerned that Americans had fallen into the habit of transferring moral and spiritual as well as political authority from the individual to his representative, and he preached a return to immanence as he urged each hearer to reclaim authority over his life. Emerson's doctrine of self-reliance did not necessarily oppose the individual to the state, but it did separate literary from political culture, realigning them in a relationship that would prove, more often than not, to be adversarial. The immanence that print had dismissed in the early national period when it had also banished the private and the hidden returned as American writers, monitored by the wild man in the margin, explored ways to simulate its effects in print.

AFTERWORD

At the conclusion of the first chapter I remarked that to arrive at a sense of another day is to interrogate today. More particularly, I suggested that an examination of writings from the early national period, when literary had not yet separated from political culture, bears on the contemporary contention that to distinguish certain writings as "literature," let alone to assert that within that category a relative few are aesthetically superior, is to affirm a position of cultural elitism and so of political conservatism. As influential writers in the 1790s took literature to include all written knowledge, so influential writers in the 1990s take literature to include all the various sign-systems in our society. If, then, the period about which I wrote saw the emergence of literature as a separate kind of written discourse, that in which I write sees it as dissolved in the cauldron of signifying practices.

Since in the preceding pages I was concerned with a range of writings other than belles lettres, and, implicitly at least, I maintained what I believe to be a liberal political view, it must be apparent that I disagree with those who treat literature as if it were an apolitical embodiment of timeless truths. I recognize the ways in which a literary work advances ideology by representing arbitrary social circumstances as an inevitable natural condition, and had I not recognized it prior to my present study then certainly I would have learned it from such explicit remarks as John Adams's on the role the fine arts play in enforcing political and religious superstitions. My sympathy with the republican idealism of Jefferson and the literary egalitarianism of Franklin has kept me alert to the assumptions of social superiority and the potential for political repressiveness implicit in pious proclamations on the central role literature plays in preserving the values of "our" civilization.

At the same time, however, since I presumed to separate better from worse writing, bypassed popular forms such as the almanac and the street ballad, and argued that a principal criterion of literary value is the degree to which a work constitutes a complex reality, it is also apparent that I disagree with those who hold that literature is inseparable from other sign-systems. I know that the idea of literature as a separate category can be challenged by citing examples that evade it, but this does not mean that it is either incomprehensible epistemologically or unserviceable empirically. At any historical moment, of course, certain works once considered literature pass beyond its boundary while others not previously so considered pass within it. But a large core has proven remarkably stable. To be sure, aesthetic criteria can be shown to have political determinants so that a literary work may be read as an ideological communication as I myself have done, for example, with James Fenimore Cooper's *Spy*. At the same time, however, I have attempted to show that literary works grow from a depth beneath the topsoil of politics, and I have valued them for the way they reflexively embody their culture and constitute ours rather than measuring them solely in terms of whatever ideological message I have detected and decoded.

While politically a break with the past, a new start, is possible, the very backbone of culture is historical continuity. There is no contradiction, then, in a society's engaging in revolutionary politics while, at the same time, retaining its prerevolutionary cultural identity. In the immediate fever of political revolution an analogous cultural revolution always appears probable to some. But neither the American nor any other political revolution has succeeded in reforming the culture of its society to anywhere near the extent to which, or with anywhere near the speed at which, it has reformed its institutions. Some regard this discrepancy as a failure, alleging that unless the revolution is total, which is to say cultural as well as political, it is no revolution at all. On the contrary, it is my observation that revolutions that depend upon cultural change keeping pace with political changes are revolutions that are doomed to fail.

I believe the apparently consistent contention that literary and political effects are identical, or its counterpart, that they have no significant relation, either obliterates the difference between the two or obscures it with a fiction of literature's atemporal self-sufficiency. What is missing from such considerations is a sense of culture as the mediating ground upon which political ideals are made to meet the inherited practices of a society and literary conventions are compelled to adjust to radical changes in social outlook. I have tried to speak from such a ground and so, for example, have sympathized with Jefferson's view of a republican society while also recognizing the validity of Dwight's opinion that no community can be cohered without regard to the prerational sources of social identity. Although I now at the close employ the large terms *culture* and *politics,* in the detailed discussions that make up this book I centered on analogous yet more specific historical oppositions such as that between *immanence* and *representation.*

And, finally, although in this afterword I make explicit the personal interests that drew me to this book, I wish to differentiate between them, between, that is, a subjectivity such as that which inevitably informs all historical inquiry, and a subjectivity that does not just lead to historical texts but replaces them with the text of the self.

NOTES

CHAPTER 1. THE WORLD COMPLETED

1 Jonathan Edwards, *The Life of David Brainerd,* ed. Norman Pettit (New Haven, 1985), p. 101. My account of Brainerd relies heavily upon Professor Pettit's excellent introduction.

2 *Life of Brainerd,* pp. 3–4, where a number of others influenced by Brainerd are cited.

3 Some years later Clap supported the Awakening and invited revivalists to preach at Yale.

4 Jonathan Edwards, *Some Thoughts Concerning the Revival of Religion in New England,* in *The Great Awakening,* ed. C. C. Goen (New Haven, 1959), pp. 387–88.

5 Jonathan Edwards, *Religious Affections,* ed. John E. Smith (New Haven, 1959), p. 135.

6 In so saying I echo Elmire Zolla, who writes, "It is as though Brainerd had met his double," *The Writer and the Shaman* (New York, 1973), p. 48, although I disagree with other parts of his book.

7 Speaking more generally of Brainerd's attitude toward Indians, Richard Slotkin notes, "He is not seeking to make them English so much as to discover and exorcise the Indian in himself," *Regeneration through Violence* (Middletown, Conn., 1973), p. 198.

8 I agree when Roy Harvey Pearce says that for missionaries such as Brainerd "conversion was everything and civilizing nothing," and that "savages were to be converted on the frontier, apart from the immediately baneful influence of civilization," *Savagism and Civilization* (Berkeley, 1988), p. 33. But this does not preclude the fact that the missionary effort served the expansionist politics of "civilization."

9   Tzvetan Todorov, *The Conquest of America,* trans. Richard Howard (New York, 1984), p. 74.

10 This and related heresies are identified in Robert F. Berkhofer, Jr., *The White Man's Indian* (New York, 1978), pp. 25–26.

11 John Calvin, *Institutes of the Christian Religion,* trans. Henry Beveridge (London, 1953), 1:72.

12 Ormond Seavey, *Becoming Benjamin Franklin* (University Park, Penn., 1988), p. 41. Seavey's distinction between self-awareness and self-knowledge is based, as he explains, on that of Georges Gusdorf in his *La Découverte de soi* (Paris, 1948).

13 I return to this consideration in the afterword.

CHAPTER 2. THE WORLD DISRUPTED

1   The most dependable biography is *St. John de Crèvecoeur* by Gay Wilson Allen and Roger Asselineau (New York, 1987). I also rely upon Albert E. Stone's introduction to *Letters from an American Farmer and Sketches of 18th Century America* (New York, 1981), the text of the *Letters* cited in the following pages.

2   Moses Coit Tyler, *The Literary History of the American Revolution, 1763–1783* (New York, 1957), 2:357.

3   This notion of linguistic reality is derived from J. G. A. Pocock, *Politics, Language, and Time* (New York, 1973).

4   Gilbert Imlay, *A Topographical Description of the Western Territory of North America* (New York, 1968), pp. 184–85; this is a photo reprint of the third edition (London, 1797). It should be noted that Robert R. Hare in his introduction to *The Emigrants* (Gainesville, 1964), reputedly by Imlay, persuasively argues not only for Mary Wollstonecraft's authorship of the novel but also for her having written the *Topographical Description.*

5   I am in some disagreement with Myra Jehlen when she says in *American Incarnation* (Cambridge, Mass., 1986) "that the decisive factor shaping the founding conceptions of 'America' and 'American' was material rather than conceptual; rather than a set of abstract ideas, the physical fact of the continent" (p. 3). Physical facts certainly did qualify the imagined America of the immigrants, but the conceptual nevertheless succeeded the facts in modified form even as it had preceded them. Indeed, the very notion *continental* is as much conceptual as physical. When Jehlen contends that the "entrepreneurial pioneers owned the land and also identified with it" (p. 4), I agree although I believe she underestimates how quickly they were able and how often they were willing to convert real into personal property.

6   See, for example, James A. Henratta, *The Evolution of American Society* (New York, 1973).

7 Jay Fliegelman, *Prodigals and Pilgrims* (New York, 1982), p. 63.
8 Thomas Jefferson, "Autobiography," *The Life and Selected Writings,* ed. Adrienne Koch and William Peden (New York, 1944), pp. 14–21.

CHAPTER 3. REALIZING THE LANDSCAPE

1 J. W. Goethe, *Travels in Italy,* trans. A. J. W. Morrison, in *The Autobiography of Goethe* (London, 1874), 2:259–60.
2 William Gilpin, *Three Essays on Picturesque Beauty; on Picturesque Travel; and on Sketching Landscape* (London, 1794), pp. 7–8.
3 The illustrative nature of Warton's poem is stressed by Louis I. Bredvold, *The Natural History of Sensibility* (Detroit, 1962), p. 57.
4 François René de Chateaubriand, *Travels in America and Italy* (London, 1828), 1:181.
5 J. Hector St. John de Crèvecoeur, *Letters from an American Farmer and Sketches of 18th Century America,* ed. Albert E. Stone (New York, 1981), p. 43.
6 Thomas McFarland, *Romanticism and the Forms of Ruin* (Princeton, 1981), p. 11.
7 Schiller, as quoted in McFarland, *Romanticism and the Forms of Ruin,* p. 11.
8 Thomas Jefferson, *Notes on the State of Virginia,* ed. William Peden (New York, 1982), pp. 53–54.
9 Thomas Jefferson, "Travelling Notes for Mr. Rutledge and Mr. Shippen, June 3, 1788," *The Life and Selected Writings,* ed. Adrienne Koch and William Peden (New York, 1944), p. 208.
10 Chateaubriand, *Travels in America and Italy,* 1:177.
11 *Peter Kalm's Travels in North America,* ed. Adolph Benson (New York, 1937), 1:61.
12 Benjamin Franklin, *Writings* (New York, 1987), p. 843.
13 William Bartram, *Travels,* ed. Mark Van Doren (1928), p. 15.
14 Garry Wills, *Inventing America* (Garden City, 1978), p. 95.
15 Wayne Franklin, *Discoverers, Explorers, Settlers* (Chicago, 1979), p. 21.
16 This attitude toward print is discussed at some length in chapter 5.
17 Michel Foucault, *The Order of Things* (New York, 1973), p. 76.
18 Samuel Miller, *A Brief Retrospect of the Eighteenth Century* (New York, 1803), 1:235.
19 Earl L. Bradsher, *Mathew Carey, Editor, Author and Publisher* (New York, 1912), p. 18.

CHAPTER 4. GAINING CONFIDENCE

1 Timothy Dwight, *Travels in New England and New York,* ed. Barbara Miller Solomon (Cambridge, Mass., 1969), 2:329.

2 James A. Henratta, *The Evolution of American Society* (New York, 1973), p. 133.

3 Ibid.

4 *Memoirs of the Notorious Stephen Burroughs of New Hampshire* (New York, 1924), p. 48.

5 William Godwin, *Caleb Williams* (London, 1970), p. 326.

6 Benjamin Franklin, *Writings* (New York, 1987), p. 1,393.

7 Susanna Rowson, *Charlotte Temple, A Tale of Truth* (Philadelphia, 1794), p. iv. In *Revolution and the Word* (New York, 1986), and in her introduction to *Charlotte Temple* (New York, 1986), Cathy N. Davidson provides valuable information about the content and reception of early American novels in general and the novel of seduction in particular. Page citations in the text are to the 1794 edition.

8 I am indebted to an unpublished paper by Jennifer Di Lalla, "Death by Seduction, Life through Narration," which develops fully the point I here discuss briefly.

9 Ezra Stiles, *The Literary Diary,* ed. Franklin Bowditch Dexter (New York, 1901), 1:132.

10 *The Confessions of Jean Jacques Rousseau* (London, 1897), 2:156.

11 Charles Brockden Brown, *Arthur Mervyn* (New York, 1962), p. 54.

12 Norman S. Grabo, *The Coincidental Art of Charles Brockden Brown* (Chapel Hill, 1981), p. 85; Warner Berthoff, introduction to *Arthur Mervyn,* p. xvii. The name of Michael Warner, whose *Letters of the Republic* (Cambridge, Mass., 1990) appeared after the completion of my text, should be added to the small list of penetrating interpreters of *Arthur Mervyn.*

CHAPTER 5. WRITING FOR PRINT

1 Max Weber, *The Protestant Ethic and the Spirit of Capitalism,* trans. Talcott Parsons (New York, 1958), p. 52.

2 Benjamin Franklin, *Autobiography,* in *Writings* (New York, 1987), p. 1,393. Subsequent citations in the text are to this edition.

3 Benjamin Franklin, "On Literary Style," *Papers* (New Haven, 1959–), 1:330.

4 "On Amplification," *Papers,* 2:146.

5 Bancroft, as quoted in Orie William Long, *Literary Pioneers* (Cambridge, Mass., 1935), p. 122.

6 Samuel Goodrich, *Recollections of a Lifetime* (New York, 1856), 1:86.

7 Kenneth Silverman, *A Cultural History of the American Revolution* (New York, 1976), p. 229.

8 Benjamin Franklin, "Proposals Relating to the Education of Youth in Pensilvania," *Writings,* p. 336.

9 Harold Milton Ellis, *Joseph Dennie and His Circle* (Austin, 1915), p. 116.

10 Joseph Dennie, *The Lay Preacher,* ed. Milton Ellis (New York, 1934), p. 124.

11 Dennie, *The Port Folio* (14 February 1801), quoted in *Benjamin Franklin's Autobiography,* ed. J. A. Leo Lemay and P. M. Zall (New York, 1986), pp. 252–53.

12 Francis Lord Jeffrey, quoted in Lemay and Zall, p. 254.

13 Charles Jared Ingersoll, *Inchiquin, The Jesuit Letters* (New York, 1810), p. 126.

14 Charles Jared Ingersoll, *A Discourse concerning the Influence of America on the Mind* (Philadelphia, 1823), p. 11.

15 Lemay and Zall, *Benjamin Franklin's Autobiography,* pp. 245, 246.

16 Thomas Jefferson, *The Life and Selected Writings,* ed. Adrienne Koch and William Peden (New York, 1944), p. 61.

17 Michael Warner, "Franklin and the Letters of the Republic," *Representations* 16 (Fall, 1986): 116.

18 Michael Warner, "Textuality and Legitimacy in the Printed Constitution," *Proceedings of the American Antiquarian Society,* vol. 97, part 1 (1987), p. 74.

19 Benjamin Franklin, "On the Hutchinson Letters," *Writings,* p. 687.

20 Franklin, *Autobiography,* p. 1,400.

21 *The Spur of Fame: Dialogues of John Adams and Benjamin Rush, 1805–1813,* ed. John A. Schatz and Douglas Adair (San Marino, 1966), pp. 59, 64.

22 Thomas Green Fessenden, *Pills, Poetical, Political and Philosophical* (Philadelphia, 1809), p. vi.

23 Gordon Wood, *The Creation of the American Republic, 1776–1787* (New York, 1972), p. 562.

24 See Warner, "Textuality and Legitimacy" for an excellent exposition of the matter.

25 This is a major thesis of Davidson's *Revolution and the Word* (New York, 1986).

CHAPTER 6. MAKING HISTORY

1 *The Adams-Jefferson Letters,* ed. Lester J. Cappon (Chapel Hill, 1959), 2:452.

2 *Letters of Benjamin Rush,* ed. L. H. Butterfield (Princeton, 1951), 2:1,090.

3 *The Spur of Fame: Dialogues of John Adams and Benjamin Rush, 1805–1813,* ed. John A. Schatz and Douglas Adair (San Marino, 1966), pp. 42–43.

4 See Leo Braudy, *The Frenzy of Renown* (New York, 1986), for a comprehensive and acute study of the history of fame.

5 *Diary and Autobiography of John Adams,* ed. L. H. Butterfield (Cambridge, Mass., 1961), 1:8, 13.

6 *The Autobiography of Benjamin Rush,* ed. George W. Corner (Princeton, 1948), p. 23.

7   Thomas Jefferson, *The Life and Selected Writings,* ed. Adrienne Koch and William Peden (New York, 1944), p. 3.

8   Benjamin Franklin, *The Autobiography and Selections from His Other Writings,* ed. Herbert W. Schneider (New York, 1949), p. xviii. For a list of "Key Editions of Franklin's *Autobiography,*" see *Benjamin Franklin's Autobiography,* ed. J. A. Leo Lemay and P. M. Zall (New York, 1986), pp. 361–62.

9   *The Confessions of Jean Jacques Rousseau* (London, 1897), 2:156.

10 Ralph Waldo Emerson, *Essays and Lectures* (New York, 1983), p. 53.

11 *The Journals and Miscellaneous Notebooks of Ralph Waldo Emerson* (Cambridge, Mass., 1969), 7:202.

CHAPTER 7. THE PERSISTING PAST

1   Carroll D. Wright, *The History and Growth of the United States Census* (Washington, 1900), p. 13.

2   Quoted in Noble E. Cunningham, Jr., *The Jeffersonian Republicans in Power* (Chapel Hill, 1963), p. 132.

3   John C. Miller, *The Federalist Era, 1798–1801* (New York, 1960), p. 109.

4   Timothy Dwight, "Greenfield Hill," *The Major Poems* (Gainesville, 1969), p. 501.

5   Timothy Dwight, *A Discourse on Some Events of the Last Century* (New Haven, 1801), p. 45.

6   Timothy Dwight, *Travels in New England and New York,* ed. Barbara Miller Solomon (Cambridge, Mass., 1969), 2:323–24.

7   Theodore Dwight, Jr., *President Dwight's Decisions of Questions Discussed by the Senior Class in Yale College, in 1813 and 1814* (New York, 1833), p. 74.

8   Dumas Malone points to this, calling it an "irresistible impulse," in *Jefferson the Virginian* (Boston, 1948), p. 378.

9   *The Adams-Jefferson Letters,* ed. Lester J. Cappon (Chapel Hill, 1959), 2:502.

10 Thomas Jefferson, *Notes on the State of Virginia,* ed. William Peden (Chapel Hill, 1954), p. 33.

11 *The Life and Selected Writings of Thomas Jefferson,* ed. Adrienne Koch and William Peden (New York, 1944), p. 436.

12 Fisher Ames, "American Literature," *Works of Fisher Ames,* ed. W. B. Allen (Indianapolis, n.d.), 1:24. Ames had a closer connection to popular literature than his writings reveal. His father, Nathaniel, and after him his brother, also named Nathaniel, authored the annual almanac that from 1725 to 1774 set the standard for that very popular genre.

13 Barbara Miller Solomon, introduction to Dwight's *Travels,* 1:xviii.

14 The most extended narrative Jefferson did provide serves as an exception that proves the rule. Prefatory to his printing of Logan's speech, a threnody on the vanishing Indian that became a favorite recitation piece for over a

century, he gave an account of the events that led to the slaughter of Logan's family. The accuracy of his narrative was sharply challenged, invoking more controversy than anything else he ever wrote and involving him in an extended search for further evidence on the matter and to the publication of an appendix to the *Notes* in 1800.

15 Charles Brockden Brown, *Wieland,* ed. Frederick Lewis Pattee (New York, 1958), p. 39.

16 Benjamin Franklin's first Philadelphia employer, Keimer the printer, was a member of the Camisard sect, also known as the French Prophets.

17 Natty Bumppo possesses qualities that make him appear the very model of the naturally noble American frontiersman upon whom democratic faith rests. Yet if we observe his function within each of the five Leatherstocking Tales rather than his striking character alone, we find him always in the service of social aristocrats such as the Effingham family, as they oppose lower-class villains and vulgarians, or of the British army as it opposes "bad" Indians and treacherous white men. In short, he functions very much as does a feudal retainer, serving his lord and supporting the established order.

18 As, of course, preeminently came to be the case with Whitman and Melville.

CHAPTER 8. CAPTIVE LANGUAGE

1 Elmire Zolla, *The Writer and the Shaman* (New York, 1973), p. 63.

2 Thomas Jefferson, *Notes on the State of Virginia* (Boston, 1829), p. 212.

3 Timothy Dwight, *Travels in New England and New York,* ed. Barbara Miller Solomon (Cambridge, Mass., 1969), 1:106n.

4 I have learned a great deal from the work of Francis Jennings, especially *The Invasion of America* (Chapel Hill, 1975), and I appreciate the accuracy at which he aims when he designates the natives as "Amerindians" and the invaders as "Euramericans." Nevertheless, I prefer using the more available names *Indian* and *American* for these two groups and trust my context to absolve me from any implication of historical ignorance or insensitivity.

5 William Bartram, *Travels,* ed. Mark Van Doren (1928), pp. 82–83.

6 *Original Journals of the Lewis and Clark Expedition, 1804–1806,* edited with an introduction, notes, and index by Reuben Gold Thwaites (New York, 1904), 1:xlv.

7 *The Journals of Lewis and Clark,* ed. Bernard De Voto (Boston, 1953), p. liii.

8 This and all subsequent quotations from the original journals may be located under the cited date in the Thwaites edition. All bracketed words in citations from Thwaites were supplied by him.

9 *History of the Expedition under the Command of Captains Lewis and Clark*

(Readex, 1966), 2 vols. This is a facsimile of the 1814 Philadelphia edition compiled by Nicholas Biddle and "prepared for the press" by Paul Allen. All quotations from it may be located under the cited date.

10 A. L. Kroeber, "Sign Language Inquiry," preface to Garrick Mullery, *Sign Language among North American Indians, Compared with that among Other People and Deaf Mutes* (The Hague, 1972), p. xxiv.

11 This parallels the historical discontinuities promoted by certain forms of modern preservation and restoration; see John Brinckerhoff Jackson, *The Necessity for Ruins* (Amherst, 1960).

CHAPTER 9. WILD USAGES

1 *Original Journals of the Lewis and Clark Expedition, 1804–1806,* edited with an introduction, notes, and index by Reuben Gold Thwaites (New York, 1904).

2 *Filson's Kentucke* (Louisville, 1910), p. 53.

3 Charles Brockden Brown, *Edgar Huntly* (Kent, Ohio, 1984), pp. 10–11.

4 Timothy Dwight, *Travels in New England and New York,* ed. Barbara Miller Solomon (Cambridge, Mass., 1969), 2:164.

5 It is an interesting aside that of all the overseers he had, the one for whom Allen had the greatest contempt was Brook Watson, sometime Lord Mayor of London and the subject of John Singleton Copley's celebrated painting *Watson and the Shark,* 1778, whom Allen called "a callico merchant who knew not how to behave towards a gentleman of the military establishment," in *A Narrative of Colonel Ethan Allen's Captivity* (Ft. Ticonderoga, 1930), p. 34.

6 Alexander Graydon, *Memoirs of a Life, Chiefly Passed in Pennsylvania* (Harrisburgh, 1811), p. 236.

7 Herman Melville, *Israel Potter* (Evanston, 1982), p. 144.

8 *A Narrative of the Life of David Crockett* (Lincoln, Nebr., 1987), p. 43.

9 Line 33 of *Song of Myself.* Lines 12–13 make a similar claim: "I permit to speak at every hazard, / Nature without check with original energy."

10 Herman Melville, *Pierre* (Evanston, 1971), p. 302.

11 Henry David Thoreau, *A Week on the Concord and Merrimack Rivers* (Princeton, 1980), p. 329.

12 Ralph Waldo Emerson, *Essays and Lectures* (New York, 1983), p. 652.

13 Benjamin Franklin, *Writings* (New York, 1987), p. 1,374.

INDEX

Adams, John: on Franklin, 100–01, 104; on oratory, 104; on his place in historical writing, 107–11, 117; on dramatic setting in history, 108, 109; on fame, 109–10; writing of autobiography, 110–113, 115, 117, 118, 119, 124; reconciliation with Jefferson, 115–16; on the arts, 134–35, 194
—works: *Diary and Autobiography of John Adams*, 110, 112–13
Adams, John Quincy, 182
Allen, Ethan, 60, 182–86, 188
—works: *A Narrative of Colonel Ethan Allen's Captivity*, 182, 183–86
America: Great Awakening in, 3–4, 12–13, 15, 16; as correlative of New Testament, 13–14; American dream, 18, 21; national identity of, 18–19, 27, 198n5; elitism versus personal authority, 32; perception of wholeness of, 37–38; progressivist discourse in, 43; history of, as undetermined by the past, 47–48; and perfectibility of human nature, 50–51, 134, 150–51; botanizing, 52–53; social mobility in, 55–58, 60–61; real versus personal property in, 75, 82, 106; as refuge, 100; political representation in, 106, 125; republican culture in, 134–38, 148; wildness in, 181–82, 184
American Revolution, 30–31, 33, 128, 134, 137, 138–39, 140, 146–47, 182–83, 186
Ames, Fisher, 136–37, 202n12
Autobiography, 17, 60, 69–70, 83, 85–90, 110–21, 124, 190
Aztecs, 11–12

Bancroft, George, 93
Barlow, Joel, xi, 94
Bartram, John, 27, 39, 40
Bartram, William, 39–46, 48–52, 158, 174
—works: *Travels*, xi, 39, 41–52
Bible, 11, 12, 13, 14, 97, 139, 155, 177
Biddle, Nicholas: *History of the Expedition Under the Command of Captains Lewis and Clark*, xii, 160–65, 167–69, 173
Bigelow, John, 120
Bird, Robert Montgomery: *Nick of the Woods*, 180–81
Boone, Daniel, 175–77, 178, 187
Botany, 38–46, 51–53
Bradford, Andrew, 86–87
Bradford, William, 86–87
Brainerd, David, 1–12, 16, 17, 197nn7–8
Brown, Charles Brockden, xii, 67–68, 76, 77, 81–82, 144–45
—works: *Arthur Mervyn*, 58, 77–82; *Edgar Huntly*, 58, 75, 178–80; *Wieland*, 75–76, 140–45
Buffon, Comte de, 38, 151
Burke, Edmund, 68–69

Burroughs, Eden, 61
Burroughs, Stephen, 58, 59–67, 69, 70–
    71, 79, 82, 94
—works: *Memoirs of the Notorious Ste-*
    phen Burroughs of New Hampshire, xii,
    59–67, 69, 79

Carey, Mathew, 52–53
Charbonneau, Toussaint, 167, 171
Chateaubriand, François René, 36, 39,
    42, 174
Clap, Thomas, 4
Clark, William, 17, 161, 163–65, 171, 172
Collinson, Peter, 40, 41
Constitution, 105, 114
Cooper, James Fenimore, 172, 174,
    175, 177–78, 181, 187, 203n17
—works: *The Last of the Mohicans*, 180;
    The Spy, 146–47, 194
Crèvecoeur, Michel Guillaume St. Jean
    de: biography of, 19–20; conclusion
    of *Letters*, 21, 22, 29–30, 33; standard
    reading of *Letters*, 21–22; irreconcila-
    ble differences within writer's posi-
    tion in *Letters*, 22, 27–29, 31; on
    harmony of farm, 22–23, 30, 31, 37;
    on free labor, 23–24; on slavery, 24,
    25; epistolary fiction in *Letters*, 25–
    29, 31–32, 36–37; on paper cur-
    rency, 28–29; on commercial world,
    29–30, 71; compared with Brown,
    81–82; on Indians, 157–58
—works: *Letters from an American
    Farmer*, 17, 18–33, 36–37, 38, 39–40,
    42, 46, 52, 119, 141
Crockett, Davy, 187–88

Decay. *See* Ruins
Declaration of Independence, 32, 108,
    109, 114–15, 116, 124–25, 155
Dennie, Joseph, 95–98, 99, 100, 161
Duplicity, vulnerability to, 56–59, 82
Dwight, Timothy: as poet, 94; interest
    in the census, 126–27, 139; political
    viewpoints of, 127–34, 150, 195; on
    the American Revolution, 128, 138–

39; interest in natural history, 131;
    on original sin, 139–40; on Indians,
    152–53, 155–57, 172; on wildness in
    white men, 181, 183
—works: *Travels in New England and
    New York*, 131, 133, 138–40, 148,
    151, 153, 156, 183

Edwards, Jerusha, 2
Edwards, Jonathan: on the Great
    Awakening, 3–5, 12–13; on the the-
    ory of providential history, 11, 12,
    13, 47; on spiritual authority of the
    believer, 13–16, 32; on grace versus
    imagination, 16; on predestination
    theory, 31; on original sin, 140
—works: *A Faithful Narrative of the Sur-
    prising Work of God*, 5; *Life of Brai-
    nerd*, 3, 5–12, 16; *Some Thoughts
    Concerning the Revival of Religion in
    New England*, 4, 12–14; *A Treatise
    Concerning Religious Affections*, 5, 16
Emerson, Ralph Waldo, 41, 125, 188,
    189–90, 191

Farmer's Weekly Museum, 95, 96
Farrand, Max, 120
Federalism, 105, 127–28, 132, 146, 182
Fessenden, Thomas Green, 105
Filson, John: *Kentucke*, 175–77, 178, 187
Fliegelman, Jay, 31
Fothergill, John, 41, 52
Franklin, Benjamin: as printer, 16, 90–
    93, 102–03, 123; on self-knowledge,
    17; scientific career of, 40, 103; and
    Bartram, 40–41; compared with Bur-
    roughs, 58, 60, 70, 82; biography of,
    58, 84, 86–88, 106; on paper cur-
    rency, 64; on appearance and reality,
    69–70, 83–84; on securing credit, 70;
    on public and private life, 84, 85,
    101–04, 124; theme of secrecy in
    Autobiography, 86; on reading, 88–90;
    on clergymen, 91–92; on lawyers,
    92; writings directed to the common
    reader, 92–93, 194; on oratory, 94–

95; and Bible, 97; Dennie's view of, 97; Jeffrey's view of, 98; Adams's view of, 100–101, 104; fame of, 100–101, 110; silence of, 101–02, 104; on publicity of writing, 102–04, 124; on plagiarism, 103–04; as representative man, 117–20, 190–91; publishing history of *Autobiography*, 120–21; death of, 121; compared with Rousseau, 122–23, 123
—works: "Advice to a Young Tradesman Written by an Old One," 70; *Autobiography*, xi, 60, 69–70, 83, 85–90, 117–21, 190
Franklin, James, 86
Franklin, William Temple, 120
Frontier and frontiersmen, 29–30, 33, 175–81, 182, 187–88, 203n17. *See also* Wilderness

Gilpin, William, 35
Godfrey, Thomas, 40
Godwin, William: *Caleb Williams*, 67–68
Goethe, Johann Wolfgang von, 34–35
Goodrich, Samuel, 93–94
Graydon, Alexander, 60, 185, 186
Green, Samuel, 96

Hamilton, Alexander, 145
Hamilton, Andrew, 87
Hawthorne, Nathaniel, 119
Hemphill, Samuel, 103–04
Henratta, James, 56, 58
History: theory of providential history, 11, 12, 13, 47; as complete, 11–12; linear view of, 12; view of American history undetermined by the past, 47–48; discrepancy in experience and written history, 107–08, 117, 118, 119, 161–65, 167–69; dramatic setting in, 108–09; continuity of, 194–95
Hitchcock, Enos: *Memoirs of the Bloomsgrove Family*, xii
Hutchinson, Thomas, 102–03
Hypocrisy, vulnerability to, 54–55

Identity. *See* Self
Imlay, Gilbert, xi
Immanence: versus representation, 15, 17, 191; abstraction of written self from immanent self, 28–29, 71; Bartram's immanent wholeness, 44–45; self-representation versus immanent self, 58, 69; women as embodiment of, 72; and nature, 85; and secrecy, 106; and autobiography, 118; and Rousseau, 121–23, 125; and Emerson, 125, 190, 191; paradox of representing, 188
Indians: missionary work with, 1–3, 6–11, 156–57, 197n8; and Brainerd, 2, 7–11, 197nn7–8; Indian prophet met by Brainerd, 8–11; Crèvecoeur on, 29–30, 33, 157–58; Bartram on, 42, 46, 158, 174; sexual behavior of, 151–52; Jefferson on, 151–55, 159, 172, 202–03n14; Dwight on, 152–53, 155–57, 172; savagery of, 153, 157, 180, 181; literary annihilation of, 153, 158–59, 172–73, 174; oratory of, 154–55; as doomed to extinction, 154–55, 157, 159; legends of, 155–57; as noble savages, 158, 174, 188; and Lewis and Clark expedition, 159, 165–73; buffalo dance, 164–65; in Biddle's *History*, 164–65, 168; communication with, 170–72; Cooper on, 172, 174; Brown on, 179–80; Bird on, 180–81; Thoreau on, 189
Ingersoll, Charles Jared, 99–100
Irving, Washington, 98, 146
—works: *Knickerbocker History*, 146; *Salmagundi*, 98; *The Sketch Book*, 146

Jackson, Andrew, 146, 182
Jefferson, Thomas: interest in natural history, 38, 42; on travels in Europe, 38–39; on commercial world, 71; compared with Brown, 81–82; on Franklin's silence, 101–02; and discrepancy in experience and written works, 107–08; as author of Decla-

Jefferson, Thomas (*cont.*)
   ration of Independence, 108, 109,
   115; on fame, 109; writing of autobiography, 111, 112, 113, 116–17,
   118, 119, 124; reconciliation with
   Adams, 115–16; as governor of Virginia, 116–17; interest in census,
   126–27, 139; republicanism of, 128,
   130, 194, 195; Dwight's views of,
   129, 130; on territorial expansion,
   130; on ignorance versus error, 135;
   Irving's lampooning of, 146; on Indians, 151–55, 159, 172, 202–03n14;
   and Lewis and Clark expedition, 159
   —works: *Notes on the State of Virginia*,
   38, 132, 139, 140, 148, 150, 151,
   152, 154, 159
Jeffrey, Francis Lord, 98

Kalm, Peter, 39
Keimer, Samuel, 86–87, 203n16
Keith, William, 87
Kroeber, A. L., 170

Labaree, Leonard W., 120
Le Veillard, Louis Guillaume, 120
Lemay, J. A. Leo, 120
Lewis, Meriwether, 17, 161, 167–70,
   172, 175
Lewis and Clark expedition, 17, 159–
   73
Linnaeus, Carolus, 39–40, 42, 43–44,
   51–52
Literature: as illustration of values of
   political democracy and literary culture, 133–34, 147–49; and republican
   culture, 136–38; as separate category
   of writing, 194. *See also* Novels;
   names of specific authors
Locke, John, 100, 140

Melville, Herman: *Israel Potter*, 186–87;
   Pierre, 188–89
Meredith, Hugh, 87
Miller, Samuel, x, 52
Mitchell, Isaac: *Asylum*, xii
Moreau, Jean-Victor-Marie, 108–09

Napoleon, 109, 189
Natural history. *See* Botany; Science
Nature: Crèvecoeur on, 29–30, 33, 42;
   wholeness of, 38, 44–45; Bartram
   on, 41–46, 48–51; usefulness of, 42,
   45–46; as ideal machine, 44; and immanent self, 85; Lewis on, 175; Filson on, 175–77, 178, 181; Cooper
   on, 177–78, 181; Brown on, 178–80,
   181; Bird on, 180–81. *See also*
   Wilderness
New-England Courant, 86, 92
Novels: popularity of, 16–17; of seduction, 56–57, 71–75; economic details
   and seduction in, 71–75; and concerns of women, 106; as illustration
   of values of political democracy and
   literary culture, 147–48. *See also*
   names of specific authors

Oratory, 94–95, 104, 154–55
Original sin, 119, 139–40, 143

Poetry, 94, 99, 105, 148
Political parties, 104–05
Port Folio, The, 95, 98, 161
Press. *See* Printing
Printing: and novels, 16–17; new readership due to, 33, 91; significance of,
   90–91, 105–06; and clergymen, 91–
   92; of legal writings, 92; personal
   reactions to, 93–94; negative views
   and misunderstandings of, 95–100;
   as guardian of civic liberty, 102; and
   Franklin's view of publicity of writing, 102–04; influence on voters,
   104–05; and establishment of U.S.,
   105; and political representation, 106
Property, real versus personal, 75, 82,
   106
Puritanism, 6, 14–15, 54, 84–85, 119,
   124, 128

Quakerism, 40

Raynal, Abbé, 151
Representation: versus immanence, 15,

17, 69, 191; imperfections of, 52; self-representation, 56–59; possible deception of, 58–59, 69, 82; in *Memoirs of the Notorious Stephen Burroughs of New Hampshire*, 60–61, 66–67, 69, 79; in Godwin's *Caleb Williams*, 68; in Rowson's *Charlotte Temple*, 74; in portraiture, 76; in Brown's novels, 81–82; impact of printing on, 94; political, 106, 125; in Franklin's *Autobiography*, 117–20. *See also* Printing

Revolutionary War. *See* American Revolution

Richardson, Samuel: *Pamela*, 16, 68, 103

Rittenhouse, David, 40

Rosa, Salvator, 175

Rousseau, Jean-Jacques, 76–77, 121–23

Rowson, Susanna: *Charlotte Temple*, 71–75, 82

Ruins: in Crèvecoeur's *Letters*, 33; European rage for, 34–37, 45, 52; lack of ruins in America, 36–37, 47, 100

Rush, Benjamin, 108–13, 115–19, 124

Sacajawea, 166–67, 171

Schiller, Friedrich von, 37–38

Science, 38–46, 51–53, 103, 131, 135, 139, 150–51

Seavey, Ormond, 17

Self: Puritan's view of, 54, 84–85; conduct as sign of, 55; self-representation as, 56–59; in *Memoirs of the Notorious Stephen Burroughs of New Hampshire*, 60–61, 66–67, 69, 79; in autobiography, 69–70, 113–14, 116–20, 122–24; in Rowson's *Charlotte Temple*, 74; in Brown's novels, 75, 76, 77–82; in portraiture, 76; Franklin's view of public and private self, 84, 85–86, 101–03, 124; immanent self and nature, 85; impact of print-

ing on, 94; Rousseau's view of, 121–23; violent self, 178–81

Sexual behavior, 56, 59–60, 72, 151–52

Silliman, Benjamin, 131

Silverman, Kenneth, 94

Sterne, Laurence, 175

Stiles, Ezra, 76

Tablet, The, 95

Thomson, Charles, 151–52

Thomson, James, 175

Thoreau, Henry David, 188, 189

Thwaites, Reuben Gold, 162

Trumbull, John, 94

Tryon, Governor, 182

Tyler, Moses Coit, 21–22

Tyler, Royall: *The Contrast*, 148

United States. *See* America

Vaughan, Benjamin, 120

Warner, Michael, 102

Warton, Thomas: *The Pleasures of Melancholy*, 35–36

Washington, George, 40, 147

Weber, Max, 83

Wesley, John, 3

Whitman, Walt, 188, 189

Wilderness: and Brainerd, 6–7; Filson on, 175–77, 178; and frontiersmen, 175–81, 182; Cooper on, 177–78; Brown on, 178–80, 181; and release of violent self, 178–81; Bird on, 180–81. *See also* Nature

Winckelmann, Johann, 35

Wood, Gordon, 105

Young, Edward: *Night Thoughts*, 64

Zall, P. M., 120